HOW TO VALUE
SHARES AND
OUTPERFORM THE
MARKET

After graduating from Wadham College, Oxford, Glenn Martin started a career in the City. Over 34 years he worked for a number of financial institutions. Having started in retail banking with Williams & Glyn's, he subsequently worked in all banking sectors, including corporate, institutional, private and investment banking. For the latter part of his career he worked as Chief Information Officer for investment banks. In 2003 he was nominated for Best Personal Contribution in the Financial News Awards for IT Excellence in Investment Banking. In 2004 he won the Banking Technology Award for the Best IT Operational Achievement.

As a successful private investor, in 1994 Glenn developed a system for calculating the intrinsic value of the FTSE100 Index and of individual UK shares. When the System proved reliable, he established ShareMaestro Limited in 2006 to package and promote the System. ShareMaestro has received very positive reviews in the financial press.

After his family and investment, Glenn's main interests are tennis, travel and drumming.

HOW TO VALUE SHARES AND OUTPERFORM THE MARKET

A SIMPLE, NEW AND EFFECTIVE APPROACH TO VALUE INVESTING

GLENN MARTIN

HARRIMAN HOUSE LTD

3A Penns Road
Petersfield
Hampshire
GU32 2EW
GREAT BRITAIN

Tel: +44 (0)1730 233870
Fax: +44 (0)1730 233880
Email: enquiries@harriman-house.com
Website: www.harriman-house.com

First published in Great Britain in 2011

ISBN: 978-0-85719-047-5

British Library Cataloguing in Publication Data
A CIP catalogue record for this book can be obtained from the British Library.

Set in Minion, Bebas Neue and FrutigerMW Cond.

Printed and bound in the UK by CPI Group (UK) Ltd, Croydon, CR0 4YY.

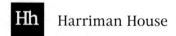

CONTENTS

ACKNOWLEDGEMENTS

The share valuation systems described in this book are based on ShareMaestro, which I launched commercially in 2007. Without the help of several key supporters, ShareMaestro would never have become available to private investors and this book would never have been written.

First I want to recognise the great work done by Zahir Virani, who turned what was a pretty crude spreadsheet into a great piece of software and who has managed subsequent enhancements very professionally. Next comes Dominic Picarda of the *Investors Chronicle*. Dominic has been a constant ally. He helped me tremendously with the validation of the share valuation system, always asks thought-provoking questions and has written some great articles on ShareMaestro for readers of the *IC*.

Tom Stevenson of *The Daily Telegraph* had the courage to headline and showcase ShareMaestro, then an unknown system, in the business section of *The Daily Telegraph*. It is extremely rare for articles on investment software to feature in the business pages of the broadsheets. Tom's article was both shrewd and positive; it sealed the launch of ShareMaestro.

Simon Griffin, although a professional chartist for *Shares Magazine*, liked the logical structure of ShareMaestro as soon as I explained it to him. He has also provided valuable assistance and advice in my efforts to get a low-cost ShareMaestro fund marketed by a fund management group.

When Dave Evans, of *What Really Profits* magazine, first contacted me to do an article on ShareMaestro, I tried to put him off because I thought *WRP* concentrated on short-term trading systems. However, Dave would not be deterred. In addition to producing some very good articles on ShareMaestro, Dave regularly suggests strategies to boost ShareMaestro returns. The use of moving averages as a key risk control for the FTSE100 high-risk strategies is down to Dave.

Annabel Watson is my model private investor. As well as acting as my guinea pig for new versions of ShareMaestro, she has put a lot of effort into the presentational side of the product. She is also a great source of inspiration.

My final acknowledgement is to my family, who provide constant encouragement and put up with my obsession to equip and motivate private investors to manage their own funds.

September 2011

RISK AND COPYRIGHT WARNINGS

Investment in equities and stock markets involves risk. Past performance is not necessarily a guide to future performance. Your specific needs, investment objectives and financial situation need to be taken into account before making investment decisions. You are strongly recommended to gain appropriate professional advice before acting on any information or valuations provided directly or indirectly by this book and to conduct your investment activity through an appropriately authorised company.

Every possible effort has been made to ensure that the information in this book is accurate at the timing of writing and the publishers and author cannot accept responsibility for any errors or omissions. No responsibility for any direct or indirect loss occasioned to any person or corporate body acting or refraining to act as a result of reading material in this book can be accepted by the editor, the Publisher or the Author.

The contents of this book, including the systems developed by the Author, are subject to copyright. These systems are restricted to personal use and may not be used in any way for commercial purposes. No part of this publication may be by any means reproduced or transmitted without the prior written permission of the publisher.

PREFACE

WHAT THIS BOOK COVERS

Buy low, sell high is an old investment adage. However, as a piece of investment advice it is useless. You cannot know, until it is too late, whether the price at which you bought will prove to be low or high. If you bought at what you thought was a low price, say 100, and the price subsequently fell to, say, 50, you can see with the glorious benefit of hindsight that the price you paid was too high. But by then it is too late. You have made a loss. To help you buy *low*, you need a system which identifies cheap prices.

The investment advice of this book is *buy cheap, sell dear*. I explain how you can calculate the real current value of the UK market and of individual shares. By comparing these values with the current market prices you can see whether the prices are cheap or dear and thus can decide whether or not to make an investment.

The principle of buying shares when they are cheap is known as *value investing*. I explain the most popular techniques that are used by investors to identify cheap shares and why I think these techniques are deficient. These deficiencies prompted me to develop my new valuation system, which calculates the current value of UK shares and the UK market. To prevent any confusion, I refer to this new valuation system as *the System* or *my System* throughout this book.

The System is different because, rather than using theoretical ratios and models to calculate the current value of a share, it calculates the current value of the two actual future sources of investment payback which the share investor should receive: the dividend stream and the sale price of the share. Uniquely the System takes into account not just relevant company-specific data but also economic factors such as interest rates, inflation and growth. This book describes how to use my System and also provides a complete toolkit for creating personal wealth through UK equity investment. It gives:

- Step-by-step instructions for creating and using the System. All you need is a basic spreadsheet. The valuation methodology is similar to that used by ShareMaestro (**www.sharemaestro.co.uk**).

- Practical strategies and techniques for using the System to outperform the market

- Advice on how to double the market value of your long-term investments purely through avoiding high commercial fund-management charges

- Recommendations of the best service providers for all the services which you need to become a successful UK equity investor at minimum effort and cost

- Details of tax breaks which you can employ to minimise or eliminate the impact of tax on your investments

- Key risk controls which you should adopt to ensure that your accumulated wealth is not damaged by surprise events

- Essential checks which you should make before investing in any share

STRATEGIES WITH A MARKET-BEATING TRACK RECORD

The book includes two FTSE100 strategies which have substantially outperformed the market over the long term:

1. A *medium-risk strategy*. In the decade ending 31 December 2010, the medium-risk strategy produced over four times the return of a FTSE100 tracker fund. Based on the long-term real annual growth rates of this strategy since 1984, you could turn £10,000 into £115,168 in real terms over the next 40 years. And you would be exposed to less risk than from investing in a FTSE100 tracker.

2. A *high-risk strategy*. Over the same decade to the end of December 2010 the high-risk strategy outperformed every commercially managed UK equity fund on the market. Based again on the long-term real annual growth rates of this strategy since 1984, you could turn £10,000 into a staggering £2,242,344 in real terms over the next 40 years.

Comprehensive long-term track records for both of these strategies are provided.

I also describe how you could transform the income payable from a fund accumulated through long-term regular saving. The traditional approach is to invest annually in a commercially managed fund or funds and use the proceeds later in life to buy an annuity (for example, to provide a pension). I explain how you could get a much higher income from a lump sum than from purchasing an annuity. I show how you could use the FTSE100 medium-risk strategy in this book to build up a fund over 45 years to deliver an annual income nearly *eight times larger* than that provided by annuity purchased from the proceeds of a median-performance, commercially managed UK equity fund or funds.

TERMINOLOGY

VALUE

In the context of this book *value* has two meanings. The first concerns what something is worth, as distinct from its price. So a house may be valued at £500,000 but be put on the market for £530,000 – its value is £500,000 but its price is £530,000. The same thing happens with shares – they can trade at prices that are more or less than their value.

The second meaning is: *market value*. The current market value of a fund is calculated by valuing all the constituent holdings of the fund at the current market prices for each holding. If I do not use the phrase *market value* in the text then the first meaning of value is intended.

FUND

In the context of investment, a *fund* is a specific, separate pool of money. A *commercially managed fund* is one operated by a professional fund management firm, such as Fidelity. These firms offer a range of different funds in which investors can buy units. The different equity funds provided by these firms cover different markets and different types of company.

When I advocate that you should manage your own funds, I mean that you should manage your own money pools for investment. Your aim is to maximise the growth of your fund(s). According to the strategies which you follow from this book, your funds may include, for example, individual shares, low-cost commercially managed FTSE100 funds and, sometimes, interest-bearing cash accounts.

WHO THIS BOOK IS FOR

This book is for anyone who wants a secure financial future – especially those who cannot rely on future earnings for a comfortable life – and for anyone who wants to take control of their own financial affairs. Entrusting your hard-earned savings to professional fund managers is a very expensive option.

To secure your financial future, you must be prepared to:

- invest up to ten minutes of your time every weekday and up to 30 minutes every weekend, if you want to use one of the FTSE100 strategies

- manage a portfolio of at least ten shares, to diversify risk, and devote on average up to two hours of effort per week, if you decide to invest in individual shares

- learn about the principles and practice of effective equity investment in order to become a better equity investor

- have an investment horizon of at least three years and not be easily panicked by short-term events

- accept some risk in exchange for the reasonable expectation of significantly higher reward.

WHO THIS BOOK IS NOT FOR

This book is not for:

- Those that believe that there is a silver bullet which will guarantee instant riches. **These 'guaranteed silver bullets' do not exist.**

- Those who trust tipsters or fund managers who, by the use of highly selective examples, give the impression that regular returns exceeding 30% p.a. can be easily obtained (for a fee!). The only professionals who abuse statistics as much as politicians are financial product salespeople. **If an investment proposition sounds too good to be true, it almost certainly is too good to be true.**

- Short-term traders who expect to make their fortunes in a few months. **Virtually all non-professional short-term traders lose money.**

- Those who want to buy shares in the hope that the company will be taken over or will realise greater value than the current market price through partial or total sales of its assets. **The system in this book does not value the assets of companies. In most cases valuing company assets is a highly subjective process and is prone to significant error.**

- Those who want to invest in shares which have no prospect of paying a dividend within the next five years. **My system uses the current and prospective dividends as the core of its valuation methodology. It cannot therefore value companies which are not expected to pay a dividend within the next five years. Furthermore, assessing the worth of such companies carries great risk.**

HOW THIS BOOK IS STRUCTURED

After the prologue, which explains the personal story of how I came to develop and market ShareMaestro, the book is divided into five parts and two appendices:

PART I – CRITICAL INVESTMENT CHOICES

Part I explains the case for investing in UK equities and why you should manage your own funds.

PART II – INTRODUCTION TO VALUE INVESTING

Part II explains what *value investing* is and the deficiencies of current approaches to value investing. I then describe the principles of the System and the superior long-term returns which you can expect from using the System effectively.

PART III – THE NEW VALUATION SYSTEM

Part III provides a step-by-step guide for you to create the FTSE100 valuation system using a basic spreadsheet. I also explain how you can use the System's FTSE100 valuations as buy and sell signals and I provide validation of these signals since the creation of the FTSE100 in 1984.

There then follows a step-by-step guide for creating a spreadsheet to value individual shares.

At the end of Part III, I look at how you can test the impact changing the input values of the System, either individually or in combination, has on valuations. This feature is very useful for constructing worst-case and best-case scenarios and for identifying one-way bets.

PART IV – PUTTING THE SYSTEM INTO PRACTICE

Part IV includes several powerful ways in which you can use the System to achieve superior investment returns. These include:

- a medium-risk, high-return FTSE100 strategy

- a high-risk, stellar return FTSE100 strategy

- a strategy for successfully running your own share portfolio

- Strategies for transforming your pension prospects

- decision tools for assessing specific investment products, including a comparison of FTSE100 investments with fixed-rate cash investment.

PART V – INVESTMENT ESSENTIALS

Part V covers essential requirements for successful equity investment, including:

- how to set your investment objectives and monitor progress

- how to take advantage of tax breaks

- recommended providers of the services which you will need

- key risk controls which you should employ to maximise the long-term real market value of your savings.

APPENDICES

- **Appendix 1**: Directory of websites which provide free relevant information for executing the strategies in this book.

- **Appendix 2**: Glossary of terms used in this book.

PROLOGUE: THE BIRTH OF MY NEW VALUATION SYSTEM

Investing is in my blood. My father was a very successful private investor and I started to read his copy of the *Financial Times* from an early age.

My experience has shown me that share investing is an essential component of successful personal financial planning. Today, because of the demise of final salary pension schemes, investing is a critical activity for most people who lack inherited wealth and wish to establish long-term financial security.

RESCUING A DERIVATIVES FIRM

In 1994, when I was working for a European bank, I was sent to rescue a European equity derivatives boutique which the bank had acquired. *Equity derivatives* are traded securities whose value is dependent on the price of an underlying share or share index. The local regulators were threatening to close the firm down because it had not submitted the regulatory returns on time and could not reconcile its trading profit with its accounting profit.

It was a fascinating and demanding experience. I got to work very closely with the traders and to understand how they made their money. I decided to study how the prices of equity derivatives are determined. Luckily the firm had a very strong training culture. There was a series of self-study tapes and text books which taught me the basics.

THE BLACK-SCHOLES FORMULA

The firm used a variation of the well-known, Nobel prize-winning Black-Scholes system for valuing derivatives. The Black-Scholes formula looks very complicated at first glance, but when you break it down into its constituent parts it is quite logical. Among the factors used to value an equity call option are:

- the price of the underlying share

- the time to expiry of the option

- the strike price of the option (i.e. the price at which you are entitled to buy the share)

- the share dividend (to which the option-holder is not entitled)

- the risk-free interest rate

- the volatility of the share price.

I completed my assignment with the derivatives boutique and persuaded the regulator to withdraw their threat to close the business down. I was then inspired to research how I could produce a system for valuing cash equities, using the same kind of logical approach as is used in the Black-Scholes formula.

A NEW VALUATION SYSTEM

Following extensive research into the way the various elements of the equities market interact, I developed the System from first principles. I completed the System in 1995 and then monitored how it performed over the next few years.

This was a very interesting period for the UK equity market. In 1997 the new Labour government withdrew the ability for tax-free entities, such as pension funds, to reclaim the 20% tax credit on dividends. As much of the market consisted of such funds, in theory the market should have fallen by around 9% because of this development. This is because the dividend yield should have increased to make up for the loss of the tax credit. Leaving aside organic dividend increases, the only way for a dividend yield to increase is for the share price to fall.

However, the opposite happened. Share prices carried on rising. Apart from a sharp drop at the end of 1998, the FTSE100 continued to climb, fuelled by dot.com mania, and reached a peak of 6930 at the end of 1999. My system said that the market was worth **over 40% less** than this. I was beginning to lose confidence in my System.

And then the crash started. Over the next three and a quarter years, when reality set in, prices fell and fell until they reached a low of 3287 in March

2003. As is usual when panic begins, market prices fell too low. By this stage, my System said that the market was now worth **over 50% more** than the price at which it was trading.

Prices then surged. They reached my valuation in less than two years – a compound annual capital increase of 24%. I regained confidence in my System. Subsequently I have back-tested the System to get FTSE100 valuations for every single trading day since the start of the FTSE100 in 1984. This period incorporates both booms and busts, including dramatic one-day crashes such as Black Monday in 1987. The back-testing validated the System. You can see the summary results of the tests in Part III of this book.

In 2005 I retired from my last employed position, as Chief Information Officer for J.P. Morgan Cazenove in the City.

MAKING THE SYSTEM AVAILABLE TO PRIVATE INVESTORS

I have always strongly believed that private investors:

- should have part of their long-term investment portfolio in shares

- should manage their own share investments rather than suffer the high charges levied by the professionals.

With the major pension changes that were introduced in April 2006 – such as employees being given for the first time the same rights as self-employed persons to manage their own Self-Invested Personal Pensions (SIPPs) and to enjoy the associated tax benefits – I saw an opportunity for private investors to use the System which I had developed to get effective returns from both SIPP and non-SIPP portfolios.

By 2007 the System had been professionally packaged and was ready to go to market via a website which I had designed. I contacted Tom Stevenson of *The Daily Telegraph* to demonstrate the System to him. I had always respected his columns for their shrewd and incisive advice for personal investors. I visited Tom in the *Telegraph*'s new premises in Victoria Plaza – ironically the very same premises where I had worked as European Technology Head for the investment bank, Salomon Brothers.

Tom was impressed by the System, which I had branded ShareMaestro. I was very pleased when he said that he would write a feature on it for the *Telegraph*. I was delighted when I opened my *Telegraph* one morning to find that

ShareMaestro was headlined in the Business Section. Tom had written a great article, which included the memorable quote: 'ShareMaestro ticks all the right boxes in my holy grail quest.' ShareMaestro was born!

Since *The Daily Telegraph* article, ShareMaestro has received very favourable reviews in finance periodicals such as the *Investors Chronicle*, *Shares Magazine* and *What Really Profits* magazine. It also featured in David Stevenson's book, *Smarter Stock Picking*, published by the *Financial Times* in November 2010.

THE VALUATION SYSTEM IN THIS BOOK

The system described in this book uses a very similar valuation methodology to that of ShareMaestro. Where there are differences, I point them out in the relevant sections of the book. The system will produce valuations which are very similar to those of ShareMaestro, except when you have chosen to use one of the alternative options which I provide for calculating a judgement-based input value (e.g. the risk premium for a share valuation).

You may ask, therefore, why I have written this book and revealed the valuation system behind ShareMaestro. There are three simple answers:

1. Although the valuation methodology is copyright, the valuation principles have never been secret. From the outset the ShareMaestro website has included a page entitled 'How ShareMaestro Works'.

2. Providing more detail about the valuation methodology and its track record prevents ShareMaestro being treated as a black box system which demands blind faith from its users.

3. The latest version of ShareMaestro contains new time-saving features that are of enormous benefit to the serious private investor, above and beyond the valuation methodology itself. You will be perfectly able to produce accurate valuations to help with your investment decisions using the System in this book, but the enhanced features of ShareMaestro will save any serious investor a lot of time.

To read more about all the features of ShareMaestro please visit the ShareMaestro website (www.sharemaestro.co.uk).

PART I

CRITICAL INVESTMENT CHOICES

The purpose of this book is to show how you can create personal wealth through effective long-term investing. To maximise investment growth, there are three critical requirements:

1. Invest where there is the greatest probability of achieving the best returns.

2. Ensure that your capital is not eroded by third-party management charges (i.e. manage your own investments).

3. Minimise or eliminate the impact of tax on your capital.

The first two requirements are covered in Part I. Ways to eliminate or minimise the impact of tax on your capital are covered in Part V, chapter 19.

1 ASSET SELECTION – CHOOSING EQUITIES

There is a wide variation in the returns achieved by different types of asset and so achieving the best investment performance relies on optimum asset selection. As an investor, you have a choice of various asset classes:

- cash (deposits in banks and building societies)

- government bonds

- corporate bonds

- equities

- index-linked investments

- commodities

- property

- alternative investments (such as art or fine wines)

- international investments.

The last four asset categories listed are outside the scope of this book, for the following reasons:

- *Commodities* are generally short-term and high-risk investments. Except for the companies listed on the London Stock Exchange where the main revenue comes from commodities (e.g. oil and mining companies), commodity investments are beyond the focus of this book.

- *Property* (residential and commercial). Except for the fabulously wealthy, the main avenue for direct property investment for the private investor has been buy-to-let property financed by a mortgage. Certainly buy-to-let property has been a very successful investment for some private investors. It has also been a very bad investment for others. This is a field which requires much specialist expertise and, in the management of the properties, a much greater investment of time than is envisaged by this book for running an equity portfolio.

- *Alternative investments.* Again this is a field which requires a high degree of specialist knowledge for successful investment.

- *International investments* carry an extra layer of risk in the form of currency risk. Adverse movements of the asset currency against the pound sterling could erode or even eliminate any gains made in the currency asset value. For this reason, we do not look at these assets here.

THE OUTPERFORMANCE OF OTHER ASSETS BY EQUITIES

That leaves the first five categories of investment in the list – cash, government bonds, corporate bonds, equities and index-linked products. For long-term investment, equities are much more likely to provide a better return than the other four options.

Investment in cash has the worst track record. Cash might have the superficial attraction of maintaining or increasing the nominal value of your capital (assuming the deposit-holding bank does not go bust and your deposit is not greater than the limit of the Financial Services Authoriry (FSA) compensation scheme). But maintaining the nominal value of your capital is a futile objective.

You are far more likely to increase the real value of your capital through effective long-term investment in equities than through investing long term in cash. For example, as shown in Table 1.1, over 50 years equities have produced over triple the annual real return of cash.

Table 1.1 – Real UK asset returns from 1899 to end-2010 (% p.a.)

	10 years	20 years	50 years	111 years
Equities	0.6	6	5.4	5.1
Gilts	2.4	5.8	2.5	1.2
Corporate bonds	2.1	N/A	N/A	N/A
Index-linked	2.1	4.3	N/A	N/A
Cash	1.1	2.6	1.7	1

Source: Barclays Capital 2011 Equity Gilt Study

Cash does play a part in the investment strategies covered in this book – but only at times when the System shows that equity prices are too expensive (and therefore quite likely to fall).

Government bonds and corporate bonds fare better than cash – Table 1.1 shows that over 50 years gilts returned 2.5% annually – but have not historically provided such high long-term returns as equities.

INDEX-LINKED INVESTMENTS

If available, you could buy index-linked gilts or national savings certificates for holding to redemption. However, they would be unlikely to give a return more than 2% above the rate of inflation (as measured by the Retail Price Index (RPI)). And even that may not be entirely risk-free for you. This is because there are large variations in price increases among the many components which make up the RPI; your personal inflation rate might be a lot higher than that quoted by the RPI. This means that even if your investments in index-linked gilts do earn 2% above the rate of inflation, the spending power of your money may still be decreasing. Therefore, we need to target a higher return than index-linked products can offer.

If you buy index-linked gilts in the secondary market (after they have been issued) you suffer the further risk that the traded prices may fall as a result of rising interest rates. At the end of 2010, the benchmark UK interest rate (Base Rate) was at an all-time low. This has inflated the prices of gilts (both standard and index-linked) and has enhanced the returns for these assets. These returns are likely to fall when interest rates rise.

These low returns and added risk mean that index-linked gilts are not suited to building the long-term financial security we are seeking.

THE REASON FOR EQUITY OUTPERFORMANCE

Why have equities been such a good long-term investment? The short answer is that managers and directors are incentivised to produce real growth in their companies. Many participate in long-term share or share option schemes and directly benefit when the share price of the company increases as a result of organic growth.

Increasingly all employees of companies are being given the opportunity to participate in such schemes. One of the prime ways in which humankind obtains personal satisfaction and esteem is to introduce beneficial change. That is one of the factors which leads to the workaholic – where the employee gets more satisfaction from his corporate role than from his personal life.

Furthermore, the UK is an entrepreneurial nation, which once ran a world empire despite the relatively small population. I expect this entrepreneurial spirit to continue to drive real UK share prices higher in the future, providing high taxes do not suffocate all enterprise.

By contrast, governments, banks and companies will pay as little interest as they can on funds which they need to raise, providing they can raise the funds. Consequently there is no embedded reason for the real value of cash and bonds to increase over the long term.

The past long-term returns which I give for strategies using the System cannot be guaranteed for the future but I believe that human enterprise will continue to increase the real value of equities over the long term. So even a passive investment in a FTSE100 or FTSE250 ETF (exchange-traded fund), with dividends reinvested, should over the long term provide much better real returns than cash or bonds. However, the ability of the System to identify underpriced market and share opportunities should enable you to achieve considerably better results than a passive strategy.

2

WHY YOU SHOULD MANAGE YOUR OWN FUNDS

The second critical investment choice which you have to make is whether or not to manage your own funds.

FUND MANAGEMENT OPTIONS

Having decided to invest long-term in equities you can choose to:

- Manage your own equity funds by running your own portfolio of shares and/or following strategies which use low-cost index-tracking funds, such as FTSE100 ETFs. ETFs mechanically replicate the performance of the index which they are tracking by holding the constituent shares of the index.[1]

- Buy units in one or more actively managed funds (e.g. a unit trust) in which the fund manager attempts to outperform their benchmark index by buying shares which they believe will perform well.[2]

- Appoint a fund manager to operate on a discretionary basis for you. With this arrangement, the fund manager has the discretion to buy and sell shares for your portfolio with the aim of maximising returns in accordance with the parameters which you have set. There is normally a minimum portfolio size for discretionary fund management (normally at least £250,000). Management fees are usually based on the portfolio value. In addition there are transaction fees for each share bought or sold.

THE IMPACT OF FEES ON LONG-TERM FUND VALUES

Due to the huge capital erosion caused by the high management charges of commercial funds, you can significantly boost your investment returns by managing your own funds.

A typical actively managed unit trust will levy a 5% initial charge and then annual charges (explicit and non-explicit) of around 1.8% p.a. Discretionary fund management fees vary but can be as high as 2% p.a.

The third-party costs of managing your own funds, using the FTSE100 strategies covered in this book, should average no more than 0.3% p.a. of your total fund. The percentage costs of managing your own share portfolio will vary according to the size of your portfolio, but should be considerably lower than commercial fund management charges.

The difference which the savings on commercial fund management costs make to your long-term savings (say 40 years) is immense, as shown in Table 2.1.

Table 2.1 – Value of £1000 saved after 40 years of annual charges (excluding investment return)

Typical unit trust (£1000 x .95 x .982^40)[3]	£459
Self-managed fund (£1000 x .997^40)[4]	£887
Extra value of self-managed fund (£887 - £459)	£428
Extra value as % of unit trust value (428 ÷ 459 x 100)	93%

In other words, assuming the same underlying fund performance, after 40 years the market value of a self-managed fund will be nearly double that of a commercially managed fund.

You might think that high charges levied by commercial funds could be justified if their performance was superior. However, commercial funds actually exhibit long-term underperformance.

THE UNDERPERFORMANCE OF COMMERCIAL FUNDS

Effective investing is about securing good long-term performance. Good short-term performance over one year counts for nothing if it is reversed the following year. Funds which boast about their stellar performance over the last year are giving you meaningless and selectively misleading information. You need to see a track record compared to the market of at least five years, and preferably ten.

Very few funds consistently beat the market decade after decade. Unfortunately organisations which monitor and publish fund performance figures do not publish figures for periods in excess of ten years. If you do look at the performance tables, the poor long-term performance of most professionally managed funds, after the deduction of charges, is striking. That is why I am so much in favour of private investors managing their own funds.

The other absolutely critical point, when looking at long-term performance, is to focus on **real returns**.

FOCUS ON REAL RETURNS

When we refer to *real* returns, essentially we mean investment returns that take account of the effect of inflation over the investment period.

For instance, if your fund has increased in size from 100 to 200 (an increase of 100%), but prices of goods and services have increased over the same period from 100 to 300 (an increase of 200%), then the real effect on the size of your fund is negative. In this example the purchasing power of your fund has declined by one-third.

ANALYSING FUNDS' REAL TEN-YEAR RETURNS

To illustrate the meagre long-term real returns achieved by commercial equity funds, Table 2.2 gives details of the ten-year performance of all the UK equity funds which had a decade-long track record in the period ending 31 December 2010 (the latest decade available at the time of writing).[5]

Table 2.2 – Comparative compound annual ten-year returns from equity funds, to 31 December 2010 (compound inflation over the decade was 2.9%)

	Nominal return (%)	Real return (%)
Median return of all commercial funds	4.1	1.2
Typical FTSE100 tracker fund	1.9	-1.0
ShareMaestro FTSE100 ETF fund	8.3	5.3
Best return of all commercial funds		
Small Cap – Marlborough Special Situations	15.1	11.9
ShareMaestro FTSE100 covered warrant fund	22.7	19.3

So the median annual real return of all commercial funds was a minimal 1.2%. And half the funds produced returns which were smaller than this; some considerably smaller – in fact negative real returns. A typical FTSE100 tracker fund, which aims to match the performance of the FTSE100 index by holding most, if not all, of the constituent shares, produced an annual return of -1%.

By contrast my FTSE100 ETF fund, which switches between FTSE100 and cash investment according to ShareMaestro's FTSE100 valuation signals, produced a real annual return of 5.3% – over four times greater than the median annual return of commercial funds.

If you were very lucky with your choice of commercial fund, you might have enjoyed the best real annual return achieved by a commercial equity fund over this period, which was 11.9% delivered by the Marlborough Special Situations fund.

However, this fund was in the higher-risk small companies sector; you would be taking on extra risk by investing in the Malborough fund. My own high-risk investment strategy – FTSE100 covered warrants fund described in this book – switches between investment in cash and FTSE100 covered warrants according to the FTSE100 valuation signals mentioned above. It delivered a real annual return of 19.3%.

IS IT POSSIBLE FOR MOST COMMERCIAL FUNDS TO BEAT THE MARKET?

One final point. Since commercial funds account for most of the turnover in the stock market, it is mathematically impossible for most of these funds to outperform the market, especially when their high fees are taken into account. Funds in aggregate cannot beat the market because, to a large extent, they are the market.

HEDGE FUNDS

The name *hedge funds* might imply that these vehicles are low risk because they hedge risk. The reverse is the case. Hedge funds generally employ high-risk techniques, such as derivatives and heavy borrowing (leverage), in an attempt to produce superior returns. The alleged superior returns are the justification given for their high fees – typically 1.5% to 2% of fund market value annually plus 20% of any profits generated by the fund.

The key point to understand about hedge funds is that the use of leverage and the other techniques to increase potential profit also increases potential losses. Unless the funds use some additional proven system which outperforms the market (such as the System), they will, over the long tem, underperform traditional funds because of their high fee structure.

This explains why so many hedge funds have such a short life. There may be short-term outperformance because of the leverage and a lucky fall of the dice. But as soon as heavy losses materialise, investors withdraw their money en masse and the fund becomes unviable.

If you want a longer explanation of the deficiencies of hedge funds, I recommend that you read the excellent chapter on this topic in Richard Oldfield's book, *Simple But Not Easy*. His conclusion was 'in aggregate hedge funds are a con.'

***

Thus, commercial fund performance does not compensate for the high charges; the median long-term performance of actively managed equity funds is poor. So not only can you achieve significant outperformance through avoiding high commercial fund charges, but you can also achieve further outperformance by pursuing your own effective, self-managed strategy for value investing.

BETTER RETURNS FROM A SMARTER APPROACH

Admittedly the decade ending 31 December 2010 was a poor decade for equities, a fact which partly contributed to the poor performance of funds in that period. The FTSE100 index was lower at the end of 2010 (5899.9) than at the end of 2000 (6222.5).

But the FTSE100 ETF and covered warrant funds explained in this book achieved superior real returns, of 5.3% and 19.3% respectively, by acting smarter. They were out of the market and invested in cash, for example, when the market crashed in 2000-2002. Fund groups make no money when you are not invested in their funds and so they prefer you to remain invested at all times – they do not encourage you to exit the fund and hold your money in cash at times of market disruption.

When the markets crash, the funds advise investors to stay put, using such aphorisms as 'it is not market timing that matters but time in the market' or 'if you had missed the 20 best days in the market by being out of it at the wrong time, your portfolio would be worth x% less'. Of course what they don't point out is that if you stay in the market all the time you will also experience the 20 worst days in the market.

As well as looking at the returns of the ETF and covered warrant funds over ten years, we can go futher and look at the historic returns of these funds since 1984. These returns are given in chapters 11 and 17.

FOOTNOTES

[1] Index-tracking funds hold the constituent shares of the index which they are tracking in roughly the same proportions as each share contributes to the index market value. Therefore, if Vodafone constituted 1% of the value of the FTSE100 then an ETF tracking the FTSE100 would invest 1% of its investment capital in Vodafone shares.

[2] The FTSE index company provides a number of UK indices which comprise UK companies of differing market capitalisation values, of which the most famous is the FTSE100. For example, the FTSE SmallCap index comprises 268 companies of small market capitalisation. So this would probably be the benchmark index for a UK Smaller Companies fund.

[3] 0.982 is the annual multiplier to levy 1.8% p.a. charges.

[4] 0.997 is the annual multiplier to levy 0.3% p.a. charges.

[5] These returns include reinvested dividends and management charges.

PART II

INTRODUCTION TO VALUE INVESTING

3

WHAT IS VALUE INVESTING?

In this chapter I will explain the basic principles of value investing and the techniques that value investors have customarily employed to produce valuations of individual shares and the market as a whole.

As part of this look at what value investing is and what value investors do, I will also explain why I consider growth investing – often cited as a separate approach, different from value investing – to not be distinct from value investing at all.

You may wish to skip this chapter if you are already familiar with value investing and the approaches investors take to valuing shares.

THE PRINCIPLES OF VALUE INVESTING

Value investors believe that share prices do not normally reflect the intrinsic worth of a company and thus the intrinsic value of a company's shares. Sometimes the prices are too high; sometimes they are too low. Value investing is about buying shares for less than their intrinsic value so as to make a profit when the share price moves towards or above its intrinsic value in the future. This is the princple of buying cheap and selling dear.

Value investors also believe that, at any given point in time, you can assess the intrinsic value of a share from publicly available information. By buying shares that trade at prices significantly below their intrinsic value – shares that are underpriced by the market – you are more likely to make a profit than by just buying shares randomly. You are also more likely to outperform the market.

Once you understand the dynamics and mathematics of share values, you will appreciate that values will change according to changes in the underlying factors which determine the share's value. So it is possible that a share price can remain unchanged but can move from being cheap to being expensive because of changes to one or more of the underlying factors. Consequently, buying cheap and selling dear will not always guarantee you a profit. But it very much stacks the odds in your favour!

ORIGINS OF VALUE INVESTING

The father of value investing was Benjamin Graham – whose ideas first came to the fore with the publication of his seminal book *Security Analysis* in 1934. He wrote this book with David Dodd, a fellow professor at Columbia Business School. Warren Buffett, arguably the most successful investor of all time, is a disciple of Graham. Graham's subsequent book, *The Intelligent Investor*, published in 1949, is still a best-seller amongst investment books.

Graham believed that you should only buy shares where there is a *margin of safety*, i.e. where the current market price of the share is at a substantial discount to the intrinsic value of the share. This margin of safety inceases the profit potential from buying the share and it also provides a safety net if there are subsequent adverse changes to the factors which determine the value of the share. In other words, if the factors that determine the value of a share change against your favour after you have bought it – meaning that your initial valuation becomes incorrect – the margin of safety gives you some protection and means you may still have bought the share cheaply, or for less than it is worth.

The principles of value investing are the polar opposite of the efficient markets theory and it is worth looking at this in a little detail here.

THE EFFICIENT MARKETS THEORY

The efficient markets theory says that, at any given time, all public information is reflected in share prices and that any attempt to second-guess or outperform the market is futile. In other words, the theory states that share prices are always fair. If true, this would at a stroke nullify the entire, mammoth fund management industry, which is based upon the ability of fund managers to outperform the market.

Fortunately for the fund management industry, and for private investors, there is strong evidence that the efficient markets theory is false. This evidence includes:

- Price bubbles and the subsequent crashes (such as the dot.com bubble and the subsequent crash at the start of the 21st century) owe more to human emotions and the herd instinct than to any sudden change in information which could justify the major price changes.

- Many studies have shown that effective value investing can outperform the market. David Stevenson's book, *Smarter Stock Picking*, gives several examples.

- The long-term successful track records of a handful of fund managers, such as Anthony Bolton of Fidelity, could not be explained as prolonged runs of luck in the casino over many decades – the odds against this repeated good fortune would be phenomenally high.

- If the markets were efficient, price movement graphs would show much straighter lines than the typical peaks and troughs. The profile would look much more like a gentle incline than a mountain range and returns would be restricted to that of the underlying economic growth.

It is very helpful to investors that markets are inefficient. The inefficiencies create great profit opportunities. However, it is one thing to pursue an investment strategy of buying shares at a discount to intrinsic value; it is quite another and much more difficult thing to determine what the intrinsic value of a share is.

Let's look at the approaches investors use to value shares. I will explain as I do this why these approaches are flawed.

TRADITIONAL VALUE INVESTING APPROACHES AND THEIR WEAKNESSES

The current approaches to share valuation fall into two categories:

A. Producing a specific intrinsic monetary value for a particular share.

B. Using indicators to find out whether the current market price represents good value. These indicators can be applied in isolation or in combination (to form a stock screening process whereby only stocks which meet specific criteria make the shortlist).

I will look at these two approaches in turn.

Later in the chapter I will look at how value investors usually value the market.

A. PRODUCING AN INTRINSIC VALUE FOR A SHARE

There are a number of methods used to calculate the intrinsic value of shares. Once a figure for an intrinsic value of a share has been calculated this can be compared with the price the shares are being traded at in the market to deduce whether the market undervalues the shares.

I have outlined the three most common methods for calculating intrinsic value here. They are:

1. Net Asset Value Per Share (NAVPS)

2. Dividend Discount Model (DDM)

3. Discounted Free Cash Flow (FCF) Per Share.

1. NET ASSET VALUE PER SHARE (NAVPS)

The Net Asset Value Per Share gives a figure for the value of a single share in a company. It is calculated by dividing the total NAV of the company by the number of shares outstanding.

```
net asset value per share = net asset value of the
company/number of shares outstanding
```

*   The total NAV of the company is total assets less total liabilities.

*   The number of shares outstanding is the number of shares issued by the company and purchased by investors.

To explain this valuation approach, I will use a very basic example of how shareholder value is created in a company.

Explaining Net Asset Value Per Share

An entrepreneur obtains capital for starting a new company by issuing 50,000 shares priced at £1 each. The shares are fully subscribed. At this stage the company balance sheet will be:

Assets	Cash	£50,000
Liabilities	Called up share capital	£50,000

The entrepreneur then uses £40,000 of the cash to buy goods and keeps the balance of the cash in reserve. The balance sheet will now be:

Assets	Cash	£10,000
	Goods	£40,000
Liabilities	Called up share capital	£50,000

Fast forward one year. The entrepreneur has sold three-quarters of the goods at a 100% profit and all clients have paid in full, creating cash revenue of £60,000. He has also borrowed £90,000 to buy some business premises (fixed assets). He still has not used the cash he held in reserve and he has banked the cash, increasing cash assets to £70,000. The £30,000 profit which he has made on the sale of the goods is taken to Reserves.

For the sake of clarity and simplicity, I have excluded other entries which the company would need to pass. The balance sheet will now be:

Assets	Fixed assets	£90,000
	Cash	£70,000
	Goods	£10,000
	Total	**£170,000**
Liabilities	Creditors	£90,000
	Called up share capital	£50,000
	Reserves	£30,000
	Total	**£170,000**

To calculate the net assets of the company, you deduct the creditors (£90,000) from the total assets (£170,000), giving total net assets of £80,000, which is accounted for by the called up share capital (£50,000) and the retained profit taken to reserves (£30,000). The retained profit is the revenue from sales (£60,000) less the cost of stock sold (£30,000), producing retained profit of £30,000. To calculate NAVPS, divide the total NAV by the number of shares issued (50,000). The NAVPS is therefore £1.60 (£80,000/50,000).

Using this method of calculating the intrinsic value of a share, the shareholders in this company appear to have done very well. They seem to have made a healthy 60% profit in one year. But would they be able to sell their shares at £1.60 each?

This is where weaknesses in the NAV approach to share valuation become apparent.

Weaknesses of the NAVPS approach

What if the remaining goods cannot be sold because they have become, say, last year's fashion? What if our entrepreneur paid too much for the premises? Adjustments to these two balance sheet items could severely affect the NAVPS.

In a mature company there are many other factors which can make it very difficult to deduce an accurate net asset value from the balance sheet, e.g.:

- Are any intangible assets that come when a business is bought – such as brand value or goodwill – at fair current value? This is almost impossible to assess.

- Have earnings, and therefore reserves, been overstated to impress the City analysts? Enron was an extreme example of this, whereby potential future earnings from contracts had been prematurely added to current reserves.

- Will debtors in the balance sheet (money owed to the company) be collected in full?

Furthermore, the company's most important assets (or liabilities!) – the company's staff and management – do not appear on the balance sheet at all.

Most companies have a net asset value far below their share price, because the market is looking at the future potential of the company rather than at its break-up value. For example, at the time of writing Tesco has net assets of £16.64 billion (also known as book value) per the latest accounts. There are 8.04 billion shares issued and so the NAVPS is £2.07p. However, the share price is nearly double this, at £4.07p. This price is influenced by Tesco's future earnings prospects and its record of unbroken earnings growth over the last five years.

The market is far more interested in dividends and earnings rather than net assets. The fact that the share prices of many companies – Tesco included – are in excess of their NAVPS figure means that this is not a useful measure of the intrinsic value of each share.

Benjamin Graham aimed for shares with a share price less than two-thirds of their tangible net asset value as a method for excluding the value of any intangible assets. He wrote *Security Analysis* in the depression following the Wall Street Crash of 1929. At that time there were a lot of bombed-out companies which met this criterion; now there are very few.

2. DIVIDEND DISCOUNT MODEL (DDM)

The Dividend Discount Model (DDM) values a share by reference to its future dividend stream. The dividends are treated as the total return which a shareholder receives through holding shares in the company.

It is necessary to assume a long-term dividend growth rate to project the future stream of dividends. This stream of dividends is then, using Discounted Cash Flow (DCF), discounted back to a present value. This present value is compared with the current market price to assess whether the price is cheap or expensive.

At this juncture I need to explain how discounted cash flow operates.

Discounted cash flow

Suppose you wanted to make a three-year investment of a £10,000 cash lump sum and you have to choose between two different products.

You know that you could simply place the money in a savings scheme backed by the UK government (and therefore treated as virtually risk-free) and simply get £11,510 back in three year's time (capital growth of £1,150 on the investment of £10,000). The sales literature advises you that this equates to a compound annual return of 4.8% p.a. We will use this risk-free rate of 4.8% as the discount rate to be used in valuing other potential investments.

The alternative is to take up other risk-free three-year savings schemes which are available. They make some repayments before the three-year maturity period, as shown in Table 3.1.

Table 3.1 – Repayments from two hypothetical investment schemes over three years

Year	Scheme 1	Scheme 2
End year 1	100	1,000
End year 2	100	1,000
End year 3	11,310	9,480
Total payments received (undiscounted)	**11,510**	**11,480**

Note that the payment streams consist of the repayment of the £10,000 capital invested and interest.

Which is the better investment? A spreadsheet can be used to make all the calculations, as I will explain when covering the System.

Here I will cover the basic principles of how DCF calculates the present value of these repayment streams.

First you need to calculate how, say, 100 units would grow each year, using a compound interest rate of 4.8%. This process is shown in Table 3.2.

Table 3.2 – Compound growth at 4.8% p.a.

Year	Compound growth calculation	Total of 100 units plus interest
Year 1	100 x 1.048	104.80
Year 2	100 x 1.048 x 1.048	109.83
Year 3	100 x 1.048 x 1.048 x 1.048	115.10

You then need to calculate the discount factor to apply to the income for each year to bring it back to present value. This is done by dividing 100 by the growth value for the relevant year. This is shown in Table 3.3.

Table 3.3 – Discount factors at 4.8% p.a.

Year	Discount factor calculation	Discount factor
Year 1	100/104.8	.9542
Year 2	100/109.83	.9105
Year 3	100/115.10	.8688

Finally you need to apply the relevant discount factors for each year to the income streams for each scheme to calculate the total net present values (NPV) of each investment. This is shown in Table 3.4.

Table 3.4 – Calculation of the net present values of the two schemes

Year	Discount factor (x)	Scheme 1		Scheme 2	
		Repayment	NPV	Repayment	NPV
Year 1	.9542	100	95.42	1,000	954.20
Year 2	.9105	100	91.05	1,000	910.50
Year 3	.8688	11,310	9,826.13	9,480	8,236.22
Total		11,510	10,012.60	11,480	10,100.92

By comparing the total net present values for each scheme, you can see that Scheme 2 has the higher net present value and is therefore the better investment.

The total undiscounted income of Scheme 2, at 11,480, is lower than that of Scheme 1, at 11,510, but the net present value is higher (10,101 compared to 10,013) because income payments in Years 1 and 2 are higher. Incidentally both schemes have higher net present values than that of the government saving scheme (10,000) which was the source of the discount rate.

The Dividend Discount Model

The Dividend Discount Model values a share with reference to the net present value of the dividend income stream, projected into perpetuity. For this model three pieces of data are required:

1. The current dividend for the latest financial year. This is factual.

2. The projected long-term growth rate of the dividend (compound annual percentage growth rate). To find this you could consult any broker forecasts available but these will cover the next three years at most.

3. The discount rate to apply to the future dividend stream which results from the above two pieces of data. This is the long-term annual percentage return which you, as an investor, would expect from investment in this share. Here it is important to introduce another concept – that of the risk premium.

Risk premium

The risk premium is the additional return which an investor would expect in order to compensate for the extra risk of investing in a share rather than in a government-backed investment, which is taken to be risk-free.

At its worst, the risk of investing in a share is that you could lose all your investment if the company goes bust. This happened, for example, to investors in Bradford and Bingley in 2008 when the bank was nationalised.

The risk premium varies from share to share, as the investment risks vary from company to company. An established supermarket chain, for example, is far less likely to go bust than a technology start-up company.

With the dividend discount model, the risk premium also needs to take into account the risk that the actual dividend stream will turn out to be substantially lower than the projected dividend stream.

The risk premium is normally expressed in terms of the additional annual percentage return which you require on top of the risk-free return. For a company, this risk premium is unlikely to be less than 3% per year but it could be much, much higher. Unfortunately the Dividend Discount Model gives no guidance as to how to determine the risk premium for a particular company.

How does the Dividend Discount Model work in practice?

First: Find the dividend for the latest financial year for the company. Apply the dividend yield (dividend as a percentage of share price) to the share price – data which should be readily available via the internet. (I will cover the sources later in this book.)

Second: Decide on an appropriate future long-term dividend growth rate percentage per year for the company in question – say 5% – and project the future dividend stream for the years ahead. So, if the current dividend were 100p, the dividends for future years, rounding down, would be 105p, 110p, 121p, 127p, 134p, 140p, etc.

Third: Decide on the appropriate discount rate. For the risk-free component of this rate, use the effective interest rate on gilts (government bonds) with over 15 years to maturity – let's say this is 5%. Add to this the risk premium rate. For this example assume that you choose 6% p.a. The total discount rate in this example is therefore 11%.

Fourth: Apply this discount rate of 11% p.a. to the above projected dividend stream in the same way that the discount rate was applied to each year's repayment in the cash investment example discussed above.

Immediately you will spot a problem. How many years of dividend income do you have to project? In theory you should project into infinity, but in practice after 50 years the discount applied to the projected dividends will be so huge that it practically eliminates the value of any further dividends.

That poses another problem – does a forecast of a company dividend to be paid, even as soon as in ten years' time, have any validity?

Fifth: Finally you would sum the present values of each dividend in the dividend stream to get the net present value of the share.

As mentioned, if the net present value of the share produced from these five steps is less than the price the share is trading at, this indicates that the share is undervalued by the market.

Weakness of the Dividend Discount Model

The Dividend Discount Model is of no practical use in calculating the intrinsic value of a share. Apart from the issues highlighted above, the model suffers from the following major disadvantages:

- It does not reflect investment reality. Investors (and especially professional fund managers) do not buy shares with a view to holding them into perpetuity.

- The model will undervalue companies which maintain a conservative dividend pay-out policy and pay out lower dividends than they could afford to pay. This is because the NPV calculation will take into account only the forecast actual dividends rather than the dividends which the company could afford to pay.

- The model gives no guidance on how to determine the critical risk premium component of the discount rate.

3. DISCOUNTED FREE CASH FLOW MODEL

The discounted free cash flow model is used to project the free cash flow for a company into perpetuity and to obtain a net present value for this by discounting this cash flow stream. The model uses the same discount rate as is used in the Dividend Discount Model.

Cash flow and free cash flow

To define what *free cash flow* is, it is first necessary to explain what *cash flow* is. Cash flow is the annual earnings of a company (broadly profits less tax paid on those profits) with non-cash items, such as depreciation and amortisation, added back.

Earnings might be paid from the company as dividends to shareholders, or retained in the company to finance future growth. Most companies do a mixture of both.

Free cash flow is more representative of the cash available for distribution to shareholders than simply cash flow. Free cash flow is cash flow less actual capital expenditure for the year. This results in a reduced figure for available cash.

Discounted free cash flow calculations

The calculations in the Discounted Free Cash Flow Model are very similar to those in the Dividend Discount Model, except that a free cash flow stream is projected for each year into perpetuity instead of the dividend stream.

This projected free cash flow stream is then discounted and summed to produce a net present value for the company. This company NPV is divided by the number of shares outstanding to produce the NPV per share.

If this NPV per share is less than the price the share is trading at, it indicates the share is undervalued by the market.

Weaknesses of the Discounted Free Cash Flow Model

The Discounted Free Cash Flow Model has similar weaknesses to those of the Dividend Discount Model:

- It is impossible to predict with any accuracy future cash flows into perpetuity.

- Investors do not buy shares with a view to holding them into perpetuity.

- The model gives no guidance on how to determine the critical risk premium component of the discount rate.

***

There are some other esoteric methods of calculating the intrinsic value of a share, but none of them stands up to close scrutiny.

B. INDICATORS FOR WHETHER THE SHARE PRICE OFFERS GOOD VALUE

I cover here the most commonly used indicators of share price cheapness and detail the inherent weaknesses of each method. These indicators are:

1. price-to-earnings (PE) ratio

2. prospective price-to-earnings (PE) ratio

3. price/earnings to growth (PEG) ratio

4. historic dividend yield (%)

5. prospective dividend yield (%)

6. price-to-sales ratio

7. price-to-cash-flow ratio.

1. PRICE-TO-EARNINGS (PE) RATIO

The price/earnings ratio is the most commonly used indicator of share price cheapness and is nearly always shown in the daily share price tables given in broadsheets. This ratio is calculated as follows:

```
PE ratio = current market price per share/earnings
per share for the latest financial year
```

- The current market price per share can be found easily on the internet.

- The earnings per share (EPS) for the last year is found by dividing the company's earnings for the last year by the average number of shares outstanding in that year.

```
earnings per share = earnings for year/average
shares outstanding
```

The PE ratio tells investors how many years of earnings (based on the latest financial year) the company will have to make in order for them to recover the share price which they have paid.

The theory is that investors will recover their investment by receiving dividends or by earnings being taken to reserves, which will ultimately increase the value of the company.

The lower the ratio, the better. A PE ratio of less than 10 is generally regarded as representing good value: i.e. the share price represents ten years of earnings.

The reciprocal of the PE ratio is known as the earnings yield percentage, i.e. the return delivered by the company as a percentage of the current share price.

Weaknesses of price-to-earnings ratio

Economic environment

The first weakness of this indicator is a theme which recurs throughout this book – you cannot assess share values in isolation from the economic environment. Whether a specific return is good value depends on what alternative returns are on offer. These returns are heavily influenced by the economic environment such as interest rates and inflation.

If inflation were expected to be 0% over the next year and you were offered a one-year cash return of 4%, you would probably regard this as a good rate, because you would expect your money to grow by 4% in real terms over the year. If, however, the rate of inflation were expected to be 20% over the next year (as it was a few decades ago) you would regard 4% as a derisory return, since your investment would decline heavily in real terms over the year.

In the same way you cannot assess whether a PE ratio or an earnings yield is good value in isolation from the economic environment. A PE of 10 which might be good value when the rate of inflation is 2% p.a. would not be good value when the rate of inflation is 20% p.a. The associated earnings yield of 10% would provide a positive real return when inflation is 2% p.a. but a negative real return when inflation is 20% p.a.

Other weaknesses

The PE ratio suffers from two further weaknesses as an indicator of share price cheapness:

- Last year's earnings are last year's news. What really matters is the expected earnings over the next few years.

- Earnings can be massaged by company management. It is human nature to put a favourable spin on bad news. Often managers are incentivised to massage the figures through participation in share option schemes. One technique is to classify high-cost events as extraordinary items so that they do not impact earnings. The ugly array of techniques is covered in detail in Terry Smith's classic book *Accounting for Growth*.

2. PROSPECTIVE PRICE-TO-EARNINGS (PE) RATIO

This is probably the favourite cheapness indicator of broker analysts.

This ratio uses the earnings projected for the current financial year rather than historic earnings. In all other respects this ratio is calculated and used in the same way as the historic price.

The prospective PE ratio is an improvement on using last year's earnings because an investor benefits from future earnings rather than past earnings. However this ratio still has weaknesses. What happens if earnings are likely to change sharply in two and three year's time? Furthermore, for industries which are known to be cyclical, such as house-building, earnings will vary greatly from year to year.

In addition, as with the historic PE ratio, this ratio cannot be interpreted in isolation from the prospective economic environment.

3. PRICE/EARNINGS-TO-GROWTH (PEG) RATIO

The price/earnings to growth ratio is used to determine a share's value while taking into account future earnings growth.

The ratio is calculated by dividing the prospective PE ratio for the next 12 months by the projected earnings growth rate for the same period compared with the previous 12 months. Consensus broker forecasts are normally used to calculate the figures.

```
PEG ratio = prospective price-to-earnings ratio/
projected annual EPS growth
```

The PEG ratio is calculated on a rolling 12-month forecast basis, so that the PEG ratios of different companies can be compared on an equal basis.

So, on 1 January 2011, the PEG ratio for a company whose financial year-end is the end of June, will be calculated from 50% of the forecast for the year ending June 2011 and 50% of the forecast for the year ending June 2012.

How to assess the PEG

This ratio has been promoted by Jim Slater in his books, *The Zulu Principle* and *Beyond the Zulu Principle*. Slater aims for companies with a PEG ratio of 1 or less. However, he advises that there should be more than one broker forecast available and that investors should check the validity of the forecasts.

He also adds several other yardsticks for screening out unsuitable companies, for example:

- Each of the previous four years must have shown positive earnings growth, with no losses.

- Gearing (the ratio of debt to share capital and reserves) should generally be no more than 50%.

- Cash flow per share should generally exceed earnings per share.

The advantage of the PEG ratio is that it is targeted on the future rather than the past. It is, however, potentially exposed to manipulation of earnings and it is only looking at earnings for the next 12 months.

Weaknesses of the PEG ratio

The major weakness of the PEG ratio is that it takes no account of the economic environment, which can significantly alter the PEG ratio of a company without any fundamental change to the company itself. This can be best illustrated by way of an example:

0% inflation economic environment

Let's take a company with a PE ratio of 15 (earnings yield of 6.66%) and a prospective earnings per share growth rate of 5% p.a. This company would have a PEG ratio of 3 (15/5) and would therefore not seem attractive, because the ratio is significantly higher than the target of 1.

10% inflation economic environment

In this high-inflation environment the market expects higher nominal yields to compensate for the ravages of inflation. Along with gilt yields and other interest rates, dividend and earnings yields will generally be higher at times of high inflation, as investors seek to protect their real returns.

In line with the market, the PE ratio of the company has reduced to 8 (earnings yield of 12.5%). Assuming it can increase its prices in line with inflation, the prospective earnings growth rate is now 15% p.a.

So the PEG ratio has now reduced dramatically to 0.53 (8/15). The company's PEG ratio now makes the share look like an extremely attractive value investment but, in reality, all that has changed is the economic environment. The comparative attractiveness of the company against other companies has not changed at all.

4. HISTORIC DIVIDEND YIELD (%)

The historic dividend yield shows how much a company pays out in dividends each year relative to its share price. It tells investors how much income they are receiving for each share they own. It is normally quoted in share price tables published by the broadsheet newspapers.

```
historic dividend yield = (dividend per share paid or
declared for the last year/current share price) x 100
```

The general idea of this cheapness indicator is that the higher the dividend yield, the better, although, as we will see, it is not that simple. The dividend is cash in the shareholder's pocket; moreover it generally has to be paid by the company in cash – i.e. it cannot be manipulated.

The Dogs of the Dow: success of a high-yield strategy

The dividend yield has formed the basis of the successful long-term Dogs of the Dow investment strategy developed by Michael O'Higgins for the US market. This strategy involves buying the ten highest-yielding stocks in the Dow Jones Industrial Average (DJIA) index of the 30 largest stocks in the US, holding them for a year and then repeating the cycle.

Over the long term, this strategy has significantly outperformed the index, although not for every year. Variations of this system have been tried for the UK market and have also proven successful over the long term.

Nevertheless, although a high-dividend yield strategy may work when applied to a portfolio of shares, it is very dangerous to regard a high historic dividend yield for an individual share as a sure sign of share price cheapness.

Difficulties with using the historic dividend yield

A historic dividend yield which is over twice that of the FTSE100 is a clear danger signal – it indicates that the market does not believe that the historic dividend is sustainable.

For example, in March 2009 Old Mutual, a FTSE100 insurance company, had a historic dividend yield of 18.8%. However, within a month the company suspended its dividend; it revealed heavy investment losses. So the prospective dividend yield instantly became 0%.

A high historic dividend yield can be misleading if the sustainability of the dividend is not taken into account. To work out the sustainability of the dividend, the dividend cover can be used.

Dividend cover

Dividend cover indicates how many times the company could afford to pay its dividend from its earnings – it is an indicator of how sustainable the dividend is. It is calculated like so:

```
dividend cover = earnings per share/dividend per
share
```

A dividend cover of 2 is regarded as acceptable as this would mean the company can afford to pay its dividend twice over out of its earnings. A dividend cover of 0.5, by contrast, would mean the company's earnings are only sufficient to pay half of its dividends. This is clearly unsustainable and a company which is paying out nearly all its earnings, or more than its earnings, as a dividend is likely to reduce its dividend in future unless earnings rise substantially. Consequently a high historic dividend yield can be highly misleading if the sustainability of the dividend is not taken into account.

The relationship between dividend cover and dividend yield

There is a strong relationship between dividend cover and dividend yields. A high dividend cover justifies a low dividend yield in the expectation that the high cover will allow the dividend to grow at a premium rate in future.

Conversely, a low dividend cover often generates a high dividend yield – when dividend cover is low, share prices fall because investors sell out of the shares. Shares are sold because investors expect the dividend to be at best kept static, if not cut; the prospect of a static or falling dividend is not attractive to investors. As shares are sold the share price drops. With a falling share price, dividend yield will increase.

For several years Lloyds TSB had a higher dividend yield than the other major banks because it had low dividend cover and had not increased the dividend for a number of years.

The relationship between dividend cover and dividend yields can be seen from the analysis of sector yields and dividend covers in Table 3.5. As you can see in the table, the higher the dividend cover, the lower the dividend yield.

Table 3.5 – Average of sector dividend yields and dividend covers (18 February 2011)

Range of dividend yield (%)	Average dividend cover
0-1	5.41
1-2	3.68
2-3	2.60
3-4	1.99
4-5	1.90
5 +	2.04 (weighted average 1.79)[6]

5. PROSPECTIVE DIVIDEND YIELD (%)

The prospective dividend yield is the forecast dividend yield for the current financial year. It is expressed as a percentage and is calculated as follows:

```
prospective dividend yield = (prospective dividend
per share for the current financial year/current
share price) x 100
```

The prospective dividend published by share data services, which I will discuss later, normally derives from consensus broker forecasts. These forecasts can be out of date. Private investors can, of course, do their own research to assess the prospective dividend yield.

As an indicator of share price cheapness, the prospective dividend yield does have the merit of looking forward rather than back.

However, it does still have two weaknesses.

Weaknesses of prospective dividend yield

1. It does not take into account any major changes which are likely to occur after the current financial year.

2. It does not take into account the economic environment. As explained earlier, the market expects dividend yields to be higher at times of high

inflation and interest rates. At best the prospective dividend yield can only be used as a comparative indicator in relation to the prospective dividend yields of other companies rather than as an absolute measure.

The next two indicators – price-to-sales ratio and price-to-cash flow – would not be used in isolation to select shares but rather in combination with other indicators in a screening process to find shares which tick all the right boxes.

6. PRICE-TO-SALES RATIO

The price-to-sales ratio is the ratio of the share price to the sales per share. A ratio of 1.5 or less is regarded as good. The perceived advantage of using SPS (sales per share) as opposed to EPS (earnings per share) is that it is less easy to manipulate sales figures. The disadvantage is that sales revenue is of no value to shareholders if it is all consumed by high costs which the company has to cover.

7. PRICE-TO-CASH-FLOW RATIO

This is the ratio of the price per share to the net cash flow per share. A ratio of less than 5 is regarded as good, although the net cash flow component of the ratio should be sustainable or even increasing, if this yardstick is not to prove misleading.

APPROACHES TO VALUING THE FTSE 100

The FTSE100 is normally regarded as the barometer of the UK market as it accounts for around 81% of the market by value. Most of the techniques which we have already covered cannot be used to value the market because they are company-specific.

Those measures which I have seen used to value the market are the PE ratio (historic or prospective) or the dividend yield (historic or prospective). These measures are very crude ways of valuing the market because:

- They suffer from the same weaknesses as I have already discussed in the context of share valuation.

- There are no accepted figures as to what constitutes fair value – such as a PE ratio of 10 or a FTSE100 dividend yield of 3%.

COMPARING THE FTSE 100 WITH TEN-YEAR GILTS

Another technique for valuing the FTSE100 is to compare the historic dividend yield of the FTSE100 with the current yield of ten-year gilts. This technique does not provide a specific valuation but it is considered that the FTSE100 offers good value if the historic dividend yield exceeds the ten-year gilt yield. This technique suffers from the following weaknesses:

- Neither figure takes account of the economic environment.

- Both figures are taken from a snapshot in time and ignore what may happen over the next few years.

The System does provide a specific valuation for the FTSE100 which does not suffer from any of the above weaknesses. I describe this system in detail in chapter 7.

VALUE INVESTING AND GROWTH INVESTING

Quite often you will see growth and value investing referred to as distinct approaches, but I believe that this distinction is false. I will explain why.

Value investors, it is said, favour stocks with high dividend yields and low PE ratios whereas growth investors favour stocks with high prospective earnings growth, which are associated with low dividend yields and high PE ratios. But value investing is just about picking shares whose present value is significantly higher than the current market price.

It does not matter whether that value arises from a *current high sustainable dividend yield* (supposedly a technique of value investors) or a very *strong prospective earnings growth* (supposedly a technique of growth investors). There have been many loss-making companies which have commanded high market prices because of their strong earnings potential, such as Amazon and Orange.

To illustrate how you can assess the present value of both high yield shares and growth shares let's look at valuing an example of each.

VALUING HIGH-YIELD SHARES

The valuations produced here assume that each share is sold in five years' time.

Company A is priced at 100p and has a historic dividend yield of 5%. Its dividend is expected to grow at a steady rate of 3% compound per year. At the end of the next five years its dividend yield is expected to remain at 5%. The prospective cash flows are as follows:

Year	Dividend increase per year at 3%	Dividend (p)
Year 1	Dividend (5 x 1.03)	5.15
Year 2	Dividend (5 x 1.03^2)	5.30
Year 3	Dividend (5 x 1.03^3)	5.46
Year 4	Dividend (5 x 1.03^4)	5.63
Year 5	Dividend (5 x 1.03^5)	5.80

The share is then sold at the end of the five years. The price the share is sold at can be found with the following calculation:

```
share price = dividend (p) x 100/dividend yield
```

Therefore, for Company A:

```
share price = 5.8 x 100/5 = 116
```

Thus sales proceeeds are 116p and Year 5 total cash flow is 121.8 (116 + 5.8).

VALUING GROWTH SHARES

Company B is also priced at 100p and has a historic dividend yield of 1.5%. This low yield is in expectation of a much higher rate of dividend growth than Company A. The compound growth rates of the dividend are expected to be 30% in Years 1 to 3, 20% in Year 4 and 3% in Year 5, as the growth rate slows down. The dividend yield at the end of the next five years is expected to be 5%. The prospective cash flows are as follows:

Year	Dividend increase per year	Dividend (p)
Year 1	Dividend (1.5 x 1.3)	1.95
Year 2	Dividend (1.95 x 1.3)	2.54
Year 3	Dividend (2.54 x 1.3)	3.30
Year 4	Dividend (3.3 x 1.2)	3.95
Year 5	Dividend (3.95 x 1.03)	4.07

The share price at the end of the five years is calculated as follows:

```
share price = 4.07 x 100/5 = 81.4
```

Thus sale proceeds are 81.4p and Year 5 total cash flow is 85.47 (81.4 + 4.07).

Assuming that both companies have the same risk premium (we could use different risk premiums if we wanted), we will assume a total discount rate of 8% p.a. (a 5% risk-free rate plus a 3% risk premium).

OBTAINING A PRESENT VALUE FOR EACH COMPANY'S SHARES

We can then apply standard discounted cash flow techniques shown in chapter 3 (pages 27 to 29) to obtain a present value for each company. I have simplified some of the cash flow timings for the sake of clarity.c

	Discount factor at 8% p.a.	Company A cash flows	Company A NPV	Company B cash flows	Company B NPV
	A	B	A x B	C	A x C
Year 1	0.926	5.15	4.77	1.95	1.81
Year 2	0.857	5.30	4.54	2.54	2.18
Year 3	0.794	5.46	4.34	3.30	2.62
Year 4	0.735	5.63	4.14	3.95	2.90
Year 5	0.680	121.80	82.82	85.47	58.11
Total net present values (NPVs)			100.61		67.62

So we can see that, based on the above assumptions, with shares priced at 100p Company A is trading almost exactly at its NPV of 101p, whereas the share price of Company B, also 100p, is nearly 50% more than its NPV of 68p.

The actual figures are not important. The point is that in conventional investment terminology Company A would be generally regarded as a *value* company whereas Company B would generally be regarded as a *growth* company. However, as we have seen, intrinsic valuations can be produced for both. Both types of company can therefore be targets for value investing. If the NPV of Company B were 150p instead of 68p, it would offer excellent value compared with the market price of 100p.

***

In this chapter I have explained value investing and described the main techniques used by value investors to identify cheap shares and to value the market. In my view, they all have significant shortcomings. As we will see, the System addresses these shortcomings to produce more reliable valuations of company shares and of the market.

Before we move on to look at how the System works, I wish to highlight that value investing is not the only approach to investing. In chapter 4 we will look at some alternative approaches to investing and some difficulties surrounding these. This will reinforce why I believe that value investing is the best investment approach, providing a good valuation system is used.

FOOTNOTE

[6] Average covers of each sector weighted by the number of companies comprising the average.

4 | OTHER APPROACHES TO INVESTING

In addition to value investing, there are two other broad approaches to investing. One is *technical analysis*, and the other comprises of a variety of methods which I categorise as *event-based investing*. I will summarise each approach and explain why I prefer effective value investing for optimising long-term investment returns.

1. TECHNICAL ANALYSIS

The techniques which are used to value an individual share or to value the market all use financial and economic data. Some of the data is factual and some is projected but all the data is used mathematically to measure the intrinsic value of a share and hence, by implication, to predict the likely future movement of market prices.

By contrast, an investor following a technical analysis approach has no interest in such financial data. Technical analysis attempts to predict future price movements on the basis of past price movements, supplemented on occasions by trading volumes. Technical analysts, or chartists as they are sometimes called, would predict the share price of, say, Barclays Bank, without knowing the name of the company or anything about its financial condition. They would just use past price and trading data to predict likely future movements in the share price.

Chartists look for patterns in price charts as predictors of future trends. You may have heard some of the expressions used, such as *Head and Shoulders, Double Tops, Double Bottoms, Candlesticks* and *Bollinger Bands* (which have nothing to do with champagne). Reading the report of a technical analyst is a bit like reading a horoscope. There is talk of resistance and support levels and of breaking out of ranges. There also tends to be a lot of conditionality such as: *this might happen if that happens.*

Despite requests I have made to several professional chartists, I have yet to see any systematic proof that technical analysis predictions outperform the market over the long term.

The only technical analysis system which I have seen to work systematically, albeit over the short term, is momentum investing.

MOMENTUM INVESTING

Momentum investing is a technical analysis technique which exploits the herd instinct, a well-known human phenomenon.

HOW MOMENTUM GROWTH IS CAUSED

As prices of a particular share start to rise, new investors will spot this and buy the share themselves. This demand further inflates prices until a wave of demand has built up, pushing the prices even higher. The trick is to invest early enough, ride the wave (letting the trend be your friend) and then take your profit before reality sets in or a piece of bad news makes it clear that prices have risen far too high and the wave crashes.

There are two other factors which fuel momentum growth:

1. Fund managers are judged by their performance against the performance of the relevant benchmark index. So, if a particular share in the index is showing strong momentum growth, fund managers will be tempted to add it to their portfolios for fear of missing out.

2. If companies in the FTSE250 (the next tier of stocks below the FTSE100) have a very strong share price performance, they may get promoted to the FTSE100. This is turn will encourage further buying as the big FTSE100 index-tracking funds will have to add the newcomer to their portfolio in order to track the index. In fact companies on the cusp of the FTSE100 often experience strong buying ahead of their promotion in anticipation of the prospective price increase.

As with individual stocks, you can also ride market momentum. Normally when market prices have risen beyond rational justification, the herd then invents some new theory to justify the sky-high prices. This is known as *confirmation bias*.

So, at the height of the dot.com boom in 1999, there was talk of a new paradigm under which dividends and dividend yields no longer mattered because technology stocks would deliver stellar capital growth through the enormous earnings potential of the new technologies. It was stressed that these companies could not afford to pay any dividends because of their large upfront capital investment programmes. On that basis, loss-making technology start-up companies were awarded valuations in the millions and billions.

THE RISKS OF A MOMENTUM INVESTING APPROACH

Momentum investing is very risky because share prices tend to fall much more rapidly than they rise. Just look at a long-term price chart of the FTSE100 (as shown in chapter 11) and you will see what I mean. Furthermore, momentum investing does not work at turning points of the market.

NEGATIVE MOMENTUM

Momentum investing also includes negative momentum, when the price trend is down rather than up. This suits a breed of investor known as a *short-seller*. The short-seller aims to make money in a falling market by selling shares at one price and subsequently buying them back at a lower price.

Identifying negative momentum is an important weapon in your armoury of risk control measures. I will explain this, and how to calculate the associated moving averages, in chapter 17.

***

If you would like to read more about the techniques of momentum investing, including the use of moving averages to spot trends, they are well explained in Mark Shipman's book *The Next Big Investment Boom*. In his book, published in 2006, Shipman correctly predicted the coming surge in commodity prices. His explanation for the prediction was rooted in analysis of economic drivers, such as supply and demand, rather than in technical analysis.

2. EVENT-BASED INVESTING

Event-based investing methods include (but are not restricted to):

- buying a share in the hope that a take-over bid will occur and increase the share price
- buying a share when it is considered that the price has over-reacted to bad news and will subsequently bounce back

- buying into a company which is issuing extra free shares to shareholders to reduce the share price from say £10 to £1 (i.e. a 9 for 1 issue) – where it is felt that the lower share price will be more attractive and will generate an increase in the new share price

- buying into a company because it has just recruited a chief executive who has a strong track record of increasing profits at previous organisation(s).

Event-based investing can succeed but it is risky because there is no logical link between the event occurring and a subsequent rise in the share price. Furthermore, often the event on which the share price increase is predicated may not occur. For example, the hoped-for company takeover may not happen. I therefore do not consider event-based investing to be as reliable an investing style as effective value investing.

5

MY NEW APPROACH
TO VALUE INVESTING

THE SOURCES OF VALUE

I described in chapter 3 what I believe to be the practical or theoretical weaknesses of the current approaches to identifying good-value shares. My dissatisfaction with these approaches led me to develop a new valuation system, one which is grounded in the realities of equity investment.

The over-riding share valuation principle is that the current intrinsic value of a share depends on what is likely to happen in the future rather than on what has happened in the past. Stock markets always look forward rather than backwards. Shares are valued on the basis of future prospects rather than on past performance. As Simon Thomson wrote in *Trading Secrets*, 'The stock market is a forward-looking discounting mechanism.'

When you invest in a share (or index), your return will normally come from only two sources, both of which are future events:

1. the price at which you sell

2. any dividends which you receive while holding the investment.

This means that any attempt to calculate the current value of a share must take account of these two fundamental factors and the System does just this.

In summary, the System:

*   calculates the future price of the share or index (in five years' time)

*   calculates the accumulated value of dividends and adds this to the future share value to determine the future value of the investment

*   reduces the future investment value by the risk premium to compensate for the greater risk of holding a share rather than a virtually risk-free gilt.

- discounts the risk-adjusted future investment value back to today's value by using, as a discount rate, the annual return on 5-year gilts (held to redemption), giving the current intrinsic value of the share or index

- compares the above intrinsic value with the current market price to establish if the price represents good, bad or fair value: the ratio of current value is expressed as a percentage, with over 100% indicating that the value is greater than the price and vice-versa.

MEASURING VALUE EFFECTIVELY

Further, in order to be effective, there are three important features that a share valuation system needs to have:

1. All calculations of a share's intrinsic value involve a certain amount of judgement. The best valuation methodology will *minimise the amount of judgement required.*

2. Also, any valuation will only be valid for a snapshot in time. Any changes to the factors which determine the valuation will change the valuation itself. It is therefore vital that any valuation system should allow the investor to *assess the impact of potential changes in the factor values to the resulting valuation.* This facility is known as *sensitivity analysis* or *scenario testing.*

3. It is also vital that a share valuation system *takes into account the economic environment* – by which I mean the current and prospective levels of inflation, interest rates and economic growth. I explained why this is so important in chapter 3. Economic growth is the total value of goods and services produced by an economy (in our case the UK). Economic growth is normally measured in real (i.e. inflation-adjusted) terms.

Previous approaches to share valuation do not meet these three criteria, but the System outlined in this book incorporates all three of these features – it minimises the judgement required; it allows one to test the impact of changes to the input factors in the valuation calculation; and it takes into account the economic environment. As far as I know, my valuation system is the only one that does all of these three things.

A FIVE-YEAR INVESTMENT PERIOD

As noted above, the System calculates the future value of a share or index in five years' time. It uses a five-year investment period to allow growth companies to grow and bubbles to burst. This period has proved consistently successful for valuing shares. It is true that many fund managers have a *churn rate* which is much less than five years – often as little as six months. However, the most successful value investing fund managers, such as Neil Woodford of Invesco Perpetual, have an average share holding period of more than five years. Five years is also the typical holding period for structured equity products (of which more later in chapter 16) and for National Savings Certificates.

DIVIDENDS AT THE HEART OF THE PROCESS

My valuation system uses the dividend as the heart of the valuation process. There are several reasons for this:

- Dividends, unlike earnings, cannot be fiddled. They have to be paid out of hard cash. A sure sign that a company is in trouble is if it reduces or even cancels its dividend or forces shareholders to accept extra shares instead of the dividend. For example, on 22 April 2008, RBS announced a decision to pay its interim dividend in shares rather than in cash. At that stage, in comparable terms, the RBS shares were trading at £3.07. Subsequently, the dire condition of the company became apparent. At the time of writing, the shares are trading at 29p.

- Re-invested dividends from 80% to 90% of the total return for a long-term value investor.

- The level of actual and expected dividends has a profound effect on a share or market price. The FTSE100 nosedived after the big banks cancelled their dividends in reaction to the credit crunch mayhem of 2008. Banks formed a significant proportion of the overall FTSE100 dividend. Similarly, in 2010, the BP share price more than halved when the company suspended its dividend in response to the Gulf of Mexico oil spill disaster. The share price only began to recover when it became clear that the company was considering reinstating the dividend, albeit at a lower level.

THE DETAILED STEPS TO DETERMINE CURRENT VALUE

The detailed steps which the System uses to determine the current share (or market) value, which I will explain fully in Part III, are:

1. Calculate the current dividend for the latest financial year.

2. Calculate the compound prospective five-year actual growth rate of this dividend by combining the expected real dividend growth rate with the projected average inflation rate for the period.

3. Calculate the projected dividend for the final year by applying the above actual growth rate for five years to the current dividend.

4. Calculate the FTSE100 dividend yield for the final year by applying a system-specific algorithm to the projected inflation rate for the end of the fifth year (dividend yields are influenced by the contemporaneous inflation rate).

5. In the case of individual shares only, adjust the above FTSE100 dividend yield by reference to the projected share dividend cover at the end of the five-year period.

6. Calculate the projected end-period share/market price, by applying the above projected final year dividend to the above projected end-period dividend yield.

7. Calculate the projected end-period investment value by adding the value of dividends reinvested over the five-year period to the projected share/market price.

8. Discount the above investment value by the risk premium. In Part III I explain the way that these risk premiums can be calculated.

9. Discount the above future value back to today's value by using, as a discount rate, the gross redemption yield on five-year gilts. I explained how discounting works in chapter 3.

10. Finally, express the resulting value as a percentage of today's market price. A percentage valuation below 100 indicates poor value and a percentage valuation above 100 indicates good value.

Don't worry if all this looks too complicated. In Part III I will take you through, step-by-step, how to set up a spreadsheet to do all the calculations. All you will have to do, when you have set up the master spreadsheet, is input a few pieces of data to get further market or share valuations.

In the next chapter I provide the long-term track records of using the System for equity investment.

THE SUPERIOR RETURNS YOU CAN EXPECT FROM USING THE SYSTEM EFFECTIVELY

In this chapter we will look at the returns you can expect from using the System effectively. I base these upon the long-term real returns that would have been achieved by ShareMaestro if it had been used since 1984 for two simple investment strategies. I will explain how to follow these strategies – a FTSE100 ETF fund (medium-risk) and a FTSE100 covered warrants fund (high-risk) – respectively in chapters 11 and 17.

As this period covers 27 years, together with several booms and busts, it is reasonable to use these performance figures as an indication of the long-term returns you can expect from following these investment strategies in the future.

THE LONG-TERM RETURNS ACHIEVED BY THE SHAREMAESTRO FUNDS

In addition to back-testing ShareMaestro FTSE100 valuations for every trading day back to 1984, I have also back-tested the FTSE100 ETF and covered warrant fund strategies for the same period. The success of these funds critically depends on the accuracy of the valuations. I provide evidence of the accuracy of these FTSE100 valuations in chapter 7.

The compound annual returns achieved by the FTSE100 ETF and covered warrant strategies since the start of the FTSE100 in 1984 to the end of 2010 are shown in Table 6.1.

Table 6.1 – the compound annual returns achieved by my FTSE100 ETF and covered warrant strategies

	Real return	Actual return
FTSE100 ETF fund	6.3%	10.17%
FTSE100 covered warrant fund	14.49%	18.66%

The returns of the ETF fund are net of average costs of 0.3% p.a. (taking account of the amount of time the fund is invested in cash). The returns of the covered warrants fund assume a 1% buy/sell spread price and dealing commission of £13 for each purchase and sale.

Comparable figures for commercial fund performance over this period are not available since these are not made available by the organisations that publish comparative fund performance data.

These returns do not take account of any tax payable. However, there are various tax shelters available, which are covered in chapter 19.

BUILDING WEALTH THROUGH SUPERIOR, LONG-TERM COMPOUND RETURNS

Once you have a method for delivering market-beating returns from your investments, you can further enhance your fund by harnessing the power of compounding.

The most common example of compounding is compound interest. Compound interest provides interest on interest after a set period, normally a year. Simple interest, however, merely provides interest on the capital invested and not on any accrued interest. For instance, £10,000 after 40 years of simple interest at 6.3% p.a. will have grown to £35,200. The same initial investment of £10,000 after 40 years of compound interest at 6.3% p.a. will have grown to £115,168.

The power of compounding applies to any percentage return. That is why reinvesting dividends dramatically transforms your long-term wealth – because you will earn dividends on the reinvested dividends, as well as on your original capital. The annual return which you receive from the FTSE100 ETF strategy consists of both capital gains and dividends when the fund is invested in the FTSE100, and interest when the fund is invested in cash. An equity investment of £100 in 1899 it would be worth £180 in real terms at the end of 2010 without dividend reinvestment, but it would be worth a whopping £24,133 *with* dividend reinvestment.[7]

Table 6.1 shows how an annual real investment of £2500 will build a sizeable fund based upon the real annual compound return of 6.3% achieved by the ETF fund since 1984. It is assumed that this annual investment rises in line with inflation. The projected fund market values are shown for 10, 20, 30, 40 and 45 years respectively.

These real returns will build real wealth over the long term. For example, the projected real fund market value after 40 years is £443,624. Table 6.2 also shows the projected inflated money market value assuming inflation of 2.5% p.a. in addition to the real return. This is the way financial institutions like to project the future market value of long-term savings plans. On this basis, the 45-year market value is projected to be £1,412,960. So, if I were using the misleading language of insurance companies, I would say *for just £200 a month, you can become a millionaire.*

I have used an annual investment of £2500 as this is 10% of the average salary of around £25,000. This is a reasonable contribution for an investor to make to a long-term pension plan.

You can easily project fund market values for other annual investment amounts or periods. So, for example, the projected 40-year fund market value from an annual investment of £1250 (5% of the average salary) would be half of £443,624, or £221,812.

Table 6.2 – Projected fund market values from using the medium-risk FTSE100 ETF strategy. Annual investment of £2500 and a real annual compound return of 6.3%

Number of years invested	Real market value of annual investment (£)	Real accumulated fund market value (£)	Real annuity payment from fund over 25 years (£)	Inflated fund market value including 2.5% inflation as well as real return (£)
45	39,078	617,188	49,665	1,412,960
44	36,762			
43	34,584			
42	32,534			
41	30,606			
40	28,792	443,624	35,699	909,575
39	27,086			
38	25,480			
37	23,970			
36	22,550			
35	21,213			

34	19,956		
33	18,773		
32	17,661		
31	16,614		
30	15,629	**221,530**	**17,827**	**368,254**
29	14,703		
28	13,832		
27	13,012		
26	12,241		
25	11,515		
24	10,833		
23	10,191		
22	9587		
21	9019		
20	8484	**100,970**	**8125**	**138,669**
19	7981		
18	7508		
17	7063		
16	6645		
15	6251		
14	5880		
13	5532		
12	5204		
11	4896		
10	4605	**35,525**	**2859**	**41,297**
9	4333		
8	4076		
7	3834		
6	3607		
5	3393		
4	3192		
3	3003		
2	2825		
1	2658		
0	2500		

Table 6.3 is in the same format as Table 6.2 but uses the past long-term real annual return achieved by the covered warrants fund, which is 14.49%. The potency of high-compound returns means that projected real fund values are very high at £1,124,879 after 30 years and £4,409,611 after 40 years. The inflated money equivalents are astronomic, for instance £10,156,052 after 40 years.

Table 6.3 – Projected fund market values from using the high-risk FTSE100 covered warrants strategy. Annual investment of £2500 and real annual return of 14.49%

Number of years invested	Real market value of annual investment (£)	Real accumulated fund market value (£)	Real annuity payment from fund over 25 years (£)	Inflated money fund market value including 2.5% inflation as well as real return (£)
45	1,102,757	**8,693,477**	**1,303,951**	22,622,383
44	963,191			
43	841,288			
42	734,814			
41	641,815			
40	560,586	**4,409,611**	**661,406**	**10,156,052**
39	489,637			
38	427,668			
37	373,542			
36	326,266			
35	284,973			
34	248,907			
33	217,405			
32	189,890			
31	165,857			
30	144,866	**1,124,879**	**168,723**	**2,037,166**
29	126,532			
28	110,518			
27	96,530			
26	84,313			
25	73,643			

24	64,322			
23	56,182			
22	49,071			
21	42,861			
20	37,436	**276,041**	**41,404**	**397,840**
19	32,698			
18	28,560			
17	24,945			
16	21,788			
15	19,031			
14	16,622			
13	14,518			
12	12,681			
11	11,076			
10	9674	**56,686**	**8502**	**66,835**
9	8450			
8	7380			
7	6446			
6	5630			
5	4918			
4	4295			
3	3752			
2	3277			
1	2862			
0	2500			

CONVERTING ACCUMULATED FUND VALUES INTO AN INCOME STREAM

As an accumulated fund could be used to provide a pension on retirement, I have included a column headed 'Real annuity payment from fund over 25 years' in Tables 6.2 and 6.3. This gives the annual payment which could be paid out of the fund for 25 years until the fund has been extinguished. The annual payment would rise in line with inflation. It is assumed that the fund investments would continue to increase in accordance with the assumed annual real returns (6.3% and 14.49% respectively).

I have chosen the 25-year period on the assumption that this would be the number of annual payments to be funded after retirement. Of course payments from an accumulated fund could be made for many other purposes than to provide retirement income.

CALCULATING THE ANNUITY PAYABLE FROM AN ACCUMULATED FUND WITH MICROSOFT EXCEL

For Microsoft Excel users, the formula to calculate the annuity payable from the accumulated fund is:

```
=PMT(return%, no. of years, -accumulated fund i.e.
the negative of the accumulated fund)
```

Where:

```
PMT = annual annuity payment which can be made

return% = annual real return achieved by the fund
expressed as a percentage, e.g. 6%

no. of years = no. of years for which annuity
payments are to be made

accumulated fund = the accumulated value of the fund
in the year when annuity payments start
```

This formula will allow you to calculate the annual payments that you can draw from an accumulated fund that is earning a given rate of return, over any number of years.

WHAT RETURNS TO EXPECT FROM A SHARE PORTFOLIO

So far in this chapter I have talked about the returns which you could expect from timely investment in the FTSE100 index. We are also going to be looking at how the System can be used to find valuations for individual shares in this book and so it is necessary to give some thought to what returns might be possible by investing in shares that are priced below their intrinsic values, as determined by the System.

Investing in individual shares carries a lot more risk than investing in an index. Individual companies have the potential to change in price far more than the index of which they form a part. Some can double or triple in price within a year, and conversely some can become worthless by going bust. That is why it is essential not to invest in just one share, as the one you pick may be the company that goes bust, but to have a portfolio of at least ten shares. You should also put into place appropriate risk controls.

Moreover, individual share valuations should never be taken at face value; further investigation is needed to eliminate fools' gold. Investor and author

Jim Slater understood the importance of this additional research and coined the phrase 'the Zulu principle' in his book of that name. By this Slater meant that the more research you conduct before investing in a company, the more likely you are to succeed. If you invested enough time researching the Zulu people of South Africa, for instance, you could become one of the world's leading experts on the Zulus. The same goes for companies. I cover the types of investigation required in chapter 13.

Because you need to investigate further the face value share valuations given by my share valuation system to find the real gold, it is not possible to provide a systematic share valuation track record of the System. However, I have on several occasions been asked by magazines to provide a ShareMaestro selection of the ten best-value and worst-value FTSE100 shares. On each occasion the selections have, *as a portfolio,* outperformed or underperformed the market over the course of the next year. Not every share in the portfolio has succeeded in these test cases, but this is to be expected.

The last such selection of ten value shares I made was for *What Really Profits* magazine. The editor reviewed the performance of the selections in the November 2009 edition of the magazine:

> 'I asked ShareMaestro to provide a top ten and bottom ten value selection in January of 2009. As of November, the top ten value have returned an average of 58% and the bottom ten value have returned 10.6%. The FTSE has returned 14% over the same period.'

Although this is just one example, it does indicate that by:

- researching companies shortlisted by the System, and
- following the portfolio management principles which I cover in Part IV of this book,

you should be able to achieve even higher returns than those of the medium-risk FTSE100 ETF strategy which we reviewed earlier in this chapter.

FOOTNOTE

[7] Source: Barclays Capital, Equity Gilt Study 2011.

PART III

THE NEW VALUATION SYSTEM

7

A STEP-BY-STEP GUIDE TO VALUING THE MARKET

In this chapter I will take you through, step-by-step, how to create a spreadsheet to calculate the intrinsic value of the FTSE100. I am treating the FTSE100 index as equivalent to the equity market since it accounts for 81% of the total market value and is, by far, the equity index most invested in by investors.

As an example I will use the valuation for 3 March 2009, when the FTSE100 reached its lowest point following the credit crunch crash. I will detail:

- each input field and where to find the source data

- each results or calculation field and the associated formulae

- the cell references for each field.

You will need access to the internet. I suggest that you bookmark the websites consulted during the valuation process for ease of access in the future.

INPUT DATA

If you are using Microsoft Excel ensure, via the Tools/Add-ins menu, that the box for the Analysis Toolpak is checked.

SETTING UP THE SPREADSHEET

Set column widths as follows:

Column	Width
A	30
B	10
C	2
D	30
E	13

You should also set the number format for each data cell, except date fields, to *number* and set the number of decimal places for displaying each number to 1 or 2.

USING MICROSOFT EXCEL

I will give the formulae in Microsoft Excel notation as this is by far the most prevalent spreadsheet in use. If you are using an alternative spreadsheet you will need to insert the equivalent formulae, or you could splash out and buy Excel; it is available from some online retailers for around £50.

I will be using Excel in a basic form. Excel can be used in various very sophisticated ways and is heavily used within the equity divisions of investment banks. If you have not got a clue about how spreadsheets work, there are plenty of books specifically on Excel (e.g. *Excel 2010 for Dummies*).

There are also very good free courses from Microsoft that teach you how to get the most from the software. You will often be directed to these if you use the 'Help' button within the Excel software or you can find them online (**office.microsoft.com/en-us/excel-help**).

ENTER INPUT FIELD TITLES INTO COLUMN A

To start, you need to enter the titles of the input fields in column A. These are:

- date
- FTSE100 price
- FTSE100 dividend yield %
- average inflation rate
- end-period inflation rate
- real dividend growth rate
- risk premium %
- redemption yield % p.a. on five-year gilts.

Your spreadsheet will then look like the one shown in Figure 7.1.

Figure 7.1 – Input fields for FTSE100 valuation spreadsheet

◇	A	B	C	D	E
1	**FTSE100 VALUATION**				
2	INPUT DATA			RESULTS	
3	Date				
4					
5	FTSE100 Price				
6					
7	FTSE100 Dividend Yield %				
8					
9	Average Inflation Rate				
10					
11	End-Period Inflation Rate				
12					
13	Real Dividend Growth Rate				
14					
15	Risk Premium%				
16					
17	Redemption Yld % pa 5-yr Gilts				
18	WORKINGS			WORKINGS	
19					
20					
21					
22					
23					
24					
25					
26					
27					

You then need to enter the input data for each of these fields in column B.

ENTER INPUT DATA INTO COLUMN B

CELL B3: DATE

Enter the date of the data from which you are making the valuation.

Entry in B3: 03/03/09

CELL B5: FTSE100 PRICE

You can obtain the price of the FTSE100 from the *Financial Times* website (at: **markets.ft.com/research/Markets/Data-Archive**).

Scroll down to the bottom of this page and, in the drop-down menus, select:

- **Category**: Equities

- **Report**: FTSE Actuaries Share Indices – UK series

- **Date**: Select the date of your choice (in this case 3 March 2009), click on the 'download' button and the report should appear as a PDF.

On the report the FTSE100 data is in the first row, with the current price shown in the second column under the date. In this case the price is 3512.1.

Entry in B5: 3512.1

CELL B7: FTSE100 DIVIDEND YIELD %

To obtain the dividend yield use the data sheet from the FT website, as produced for the FTSE100 price.

The FTSE100 dividend yield is shown under the column headed Div. yld%. In this case the yield was 5.95%.

Entry in B7: 5.95

CELL B9: AVERAGE INFLATION RATE

You can obtain the average inflation rate from the Bank of England website (**www.bankofengland.co.uk/statistics/yieldcurve**).

The Bank of England produces a daily report to show inflation expectations as implied by the prices of market instruments. Scroll down to the section headed 'Implied Inflation (Government Liability)' against an Excel icon.

Click on this wording and a dialogue box will appear. Click on OK to open the file (normally with Microsoft Excel). The file should download and appear on your screen.

Click on the 'spot curve' tab and scroll sideways to the column headed 5.00. This shows the average inflation expected over the next five years. Read across from the required date on the left (normally the last date if you are doing a current valuation) to get the appropriate figure under the column headed 5.00.

Normally there is a time-lag of one working day in this data being updated. Don't worry if you have to use the previous day's figure as there is normally very little change in the figure over one day.

I do not advise using the System if either the average or end-period inflation rate is over 10.5%. In the case of this example, the figure shown is 1.5%.

Entry in B9: 1.5

CELL B11: END-PERIOD INFLATION RATE

The source for the end-period inflation rate is the same as above for average inflation rate.

Click on the 'fwd curve' tab and scroll sideways to the column headed 5.00. This shows the inflation rate expected at the end of the next five years. Read across from the required date on the left (normally the last date if you are doing a current valuation) to get the appropriate figure under the column headed 5.00.

Normally there is a time-lag of one working day in this data being updated. Don't worry if you have to use the previous day's figure as there is normally very little change in the figure over one day.

In our example, the figure shown in the spreadsheet is 3.25%.

Entry in B11: 3.25

CELL B13: REAL DIVIDEND GROWTH RATE

The expected real dividend growth rate is a critical element in determining the FTSE100 valuation. It is the real compound growth rate percentage expected per year in the FTSE100 dividend over the next five years. There is no source for this. It is assessed by judgement.

Table 7.1 shows the real annual dividend growth rates of the FTSE100 since 1986, the first year for which reliable FTSE100 dividend yields are available. This table is based on the weighted average net dividend actually paid by companies comprising the FTSE100. The weighting is according to the market capitalisation of the companies at the time.

When non-taxpayers, including institutions, could claim back the tax credit attached to dividends, dividend yields were normally quoted including the tax credit. The ability to reclaim the tax credit was abolished in 1997 and so I have used the net dividend figure to avoid distortions in the year-on-year growth rate calculations.

It is unlikely that you will have seen such a data table anywhere else. Normally insufficient attention is paid to the FTSE100 dividend growth. The table shows that real annual five-year growth rates of the FTSE100 net dividend have varied from 7.5% p.a. to -2.9% p.a. The average compound annual percentage increase over the whole period equates to 2.1%.

After Table 7.1 I will explain how to determine a value for this critical figure.

Table 7.1 – FTSE100 five-year dividend growth 1986-2010

Date	FTSE100 price	FTSE100 net dividend	Net dividend compound p.a. actual increase on five years ago (%)	Retail Price Index (RPI) compound p.a. increase on five years ago (%)	Net dividend compound p.a. real increase on five years ago (%)
02/01/1986	1420.5	44.7			
02/01/1987	1681.1	49.4			
04/01/1988	1747.5	57.4			
03/01/1989	1782.8	67.8			
02/01/1990	2434.1	76.3			
02/01/1991	2128.3	87.0	14.2	6.2	7.5
02/01/1992	2492.8	91.6	13.1	6.3	6.5
04/01/1993	2861.5	89.9	9.4	5.9	3.2
04/01/1994	3408.5	97.3	7.5	4.9	2.4
03/01/1995	3065.7	103.3	6.2	4.1	2.1
02/01/1996	3687.9	115.1	5.7	2.9	2.8
02/01/1997	4057.4	127.9	6.9	2.6	4.2
02/01/1998	5193.5	130.0	7.7	3.0	4.6
04/01/1999	5879.4	139.9	7.5	2.9	4.4
04/01/2000	6665.9	141.3	6.5	2.7	3.7
02/01/2001	6174.7	134.6	3.2	2.6	0.5
02/01/2002	5218.3	135.2	1.1	2.3	-1.2
02/01/2003	4009.5	139.9	1.5	2.3	-0.8
02/01/2004	4510.2	143.0	0.4	2.3	-1.8
04/01/2005	4847.0	152.2	1.5	2.5	-1.0
03/01/2006	5681.5	173.9	5.2	2.5	2.7
02/01/2007	6310.9	190.6	7.1	3.1	3.9
02/01/2008	6416.7	202.1	7.6	3.3	4.2
02/01/2009	4561.8	196.6	6.6	2.8	3.7
04/01/2010	5500.3	178.8	3.3	2.9	0.4
04/01/2011	6013.9	176.8	0.3	3.4	-2.9
Compound growth over whole period (% p.a.)			**Actual dividend**	**RPI**	**Real dividend**
			5.7	3.5	2.1

How to determine what real dividend growth rate to use

In normal times, in the absence of any more convincing information, I would use 2% p.a. as the default real dividend growth rate for the FTSE100. This is very close to the long-term FTSE100 real dividend growth rate of 2.06% p.a.

However, times were far from normal on 3 March 2009. The UK was in the grip of the most severe recession since World War II. The consensus amongst analysts was that dividends would be cut by 30% over the coming year. Accepting this consensus for Year 1, I projected that dividends would remain static in real terms in Year 2 and then resume 2% real growth for Years 3, 4 and 5.

If the period starts with a real dividend of 100, the dividend will reduce to 70 in nominal terms in Year 1, because of the 30% cut. In real terms the figure is lower, because of the expected inflation of 1.5% p.a. To reduce 70 to the real value at the end of the first year you multiply 70 by 100/101.5, which gives 68.97.

Given my above assumptions, the equation to get the projected real value of the dividend at the end of Year 5 is:

```
68.97 x 1 x 1.02 x 1.02 x 1.02 = 73.19
```

In this equation you can see I have assumed no growth in the dividend in Year 2 (x 1) and a 2% growth in Years 3, 4 and 5 (x 1.02).

How do you calculate the compound real dividend growth rate over the five-year period, with a starting value of 100 and an end value of 73.19? Here Excel comes to the rescue.

There is a special formula which calculates the growth rate. You can include this formula in the workings section of the spreadsheet which you construct:

- In cell D19 enter title 'Start Date' and in E19 enter a date at the beginning of a year – say 1/1/00. **Ensure via the Format/cell menu that the Date format is selected.**

- In cell D20 enter title 'End Date' and in E20 enter a date five years later – say 1/1/05. **Ensure via the Format/cell menu that the Date format is selected.**

- In cell D25 enter title 'Real Dividend Start Period' and in E25 enter: -100 (i.e. negative).

- In cell D26 enter title 'Real Dividend End Period' and in E26 enter the projected real dividend at the end of the five-year period – in this example: 73.19

- In cell D27 enter the title 'Real Dividend Growth Rate % p.a.' and in E27 enter the formula to calculate the compound real dividend growth rate over the period: =XIRR(E25:E26,E19:E20,0.1)*100. The formula will calculate the real compound dividend growth rate over the five-year period: in this example it is -6% p.a. (i.e. negative growth). Enter the resulting value in B13.

Entry in B13: =E27

If you want to use the same real dividend growth rate for each year of the forecast (e.g. the long-term rate of 2.06) just enter this rate in Cell B13.

CELL B15: RISK PREMIUM %

The risk premium compensates for the greater risk of holding equities than of holding a virtually risk-free gilt (if held to redemption). In the System the end period investment value is risk-adjusted as follows:

```
(end-period investment value x 100)/(100 + risk
premium)
```

This is a somewhat different method from most risk premium models, which use a discount rate of x% p.a. to cater for the risk premium.

There is no source for the risk premium, as it is a matter of judgement and experience. However, back-testing my System for every trading day to the start of the FTSE100 suggests that 10% is an appropriate figure for the FTSE100 over the five-year period.

Entry in B15: 10

CELL A17: REDEMPTION YIELD % P.A. FIVE-YEAR GILTS

You can obtain the redemption yield per year for five-year gilts from the *FT* website (at: **markets.ft.com/research/Markets/Data-Archive**).

Scroll down to the bottom of the page and, in the drop-down menus, select:

- **Category**: Bonds and Rates

- **Report**: FTSE UK Gilts Indices

- **Date**: Select the date of your choice (in this case 3 March 2009) and click on the 'download' button and the report should appear as a PDF.

In the middle of the page, there are three rows under the heading 'Yield Indices'. Select the first row '5 yrs' and the value for the appropriate date. This is the compound risk-free rate for a gilt held for five years to redemption. For this example the figure shown is 2.41, so we enter this in B17.

Entry in B17: 2.41

RESULTS

ENTER RESULTS FIELD TITLES INTO COLUMN D

Having completed the input data, you need to enter the labels of the results fields into column D. These are:

- current net dividend
- actual divided growth percentage p.a.
- end-period dividend
- end-period dividend yield
- end-period FTSE100 price
- average dividend yield
- end-period investment value BR (BR = taking account of basic rate tax)
- discounted investment value BR
- projected growth for period percentage BR
- projected annual growth percentage BR
- end-period investment value HR (HR = taking account of higher rate tax)
- projected growth for period percentage HR
- projected annual growth percentage HR
- FTSE100 intrinsic value
- value as a percentage of current price.

Your spreadsheet will then look like the one shown in Figure 7.2.

Figure 7.2 – Result field labels for FTSE100 valuation spreadsheet

◇	A	B	C	D	E
1	**FTSE100 VALUATION**				
2	**INPUT DATA**			**RESULTS**	
3	Date	3-Mar-09		Current Net Dividend	209.0
4				Actual Dividend Growth % p.a.	
5	FTSE100 Price	3512.1		End-period Dividend	
6				End-period Dividend Yield	
7	FTSE100 Dividend Yield %	5.95		End-period FTSE100 Price	
8				Average Dividend Yield	
9	Average Inflation Rate	1.5		End-period Investment Value BR	
10				Discounted Investment Value BR	
11	End-Period Inflation Rate	3.25		Projected growth for period % BR	
12				Projected annual growth % BR	
13	Real Dividend Growth Rate	-6.0		End-period Investment Value HR	
14				Projected growth for period % HR	
15	Risk Premium%	10		Projected annual growth % HR	
16				FTSE100 Intrinsic Value	
17	Redemption Yld % pa 5-yr Gilts	2.41		Value as % of Current Price	
18	**WORKINGS**			**WORKINGS**	
19	Inflation Growth Factor			Start Date	1/1/00
20	Real Dividend Growth Factor			End Date	1/1/05
21				Start Investment Value BR	
22				End Investment Value BR	
23				Start Investment Value HR	
24				End Investment Value HR	
25	End-period Investment Value BR			Real Dividend Start Period	-100.0
26				Real Dividend End Period	73.19
27				Real Dividend Growth Rate % p.a.	-6.0

Let's look now at how to populate these results fields. I describe each results field and the formula which you should enter to calculate the relevant figure for the field.

ENTERING RESULTS DATA INTO COLUMN E

CELL E3: CURRENT NET DIVIDEND

This is the current dividend of the FTSE100, net of the tax credit. The dividend yield of the FTSE100 is calculated from the dividends of the 100 constituent companies, weighted by the market capitalisation of the companies. You calculate the net dividend of the FTSE100 in the same way that you would calculate the net dividend of the share. Apply the percentage dividend yield to the market price of the FTSE100.

Formula entry in E3: =+B5*B7/100

CELL E4: ACTUAL DIVIDEND GROWTH % P.A.

This is calculated by combining the real dividend growth rate (cell B13) with the average inflation rate (cell B9). First, in the workings part of the spreadsheet:

- enter in A19: Inflation growth factor

- formula entry in B19: =(1+(B9/100))

- enter in A20: Real dividend growth factor

- formula entry in B20: =(1+(B13/100))

When we have figures for the inflation growth factor and the real dividend growth factor we can deduce the actual dividend growth percentage per year. This is done as follows:

Formula entry in E4: =((B19*B20)-1)*100

CELL E5: END-PERIOD DIVIDEND

This is the projected dividend in the fifth year of the period, calculated by compounding the current net dividend by the actual dividend growth rate: 1+(E4/100) for five successive years.

Formula entry in E5: =+E3*(1+(E4/100))^5

CELL E6: END-PERIOD DIVIDEND YIELD

This is the projected FTSE100 dividend yield at the end of the five-year period. It takes into account the projected inflation rate for the end of the period (cell B11). The calculations for this yield in ShareMaestro are proprietary and complex. The following formula comes very close to the ShareMaestro value and uses the projected end-period inflation rate.

Formula entry in E6: =+(B11/10.5*3)+2.4

CELL E7: END-PERIOD FTSE100 PRICE

This price follows directly from the end-period dividend (cell E5) and the end-period dividend yield (cell E6). It is calculated as follows:

Formula entry in E7: =100/E6*E5

CELL E8: AVERAGE DIVIDEND YIELD

This is calculated from the average of the current dividend yield and the end-period dividend yield:

Formula entry in E8: =+(B7+E6)/2

CELL E9: END-PERIOD INVESTMENT VALUE BR

This is the end-period investment value assuming basic rate (BR) Income Tax is paid on the dividends. It is calculated by adding to the end-period FTSE100 price five years' worth of the average dividends, net of basic rate tax (i.e. the net dividend paid by the company):

Formula entry in E9: =+E7*((1+(E8/100))^5)

This formula would need to be altered if a change to tax affected the amount of the net dividend paid by the company which is payable to a basic-rate taxpayer. Currently a basic-rate taxpayer receives the full dividend paid by the company and does not need to pay any further tax on it.

CELL E10: DISCOUNTED INVESTMENT VALUE BR

This value is calculated by discounting the projected investment value with BR tax (in five years' time) back to today's value by using, as a discount rate, the gross annual yield on five-year gilts held in redemption.

To calculate the discounted present value of the end-period investment value, you need to set up some formulae in the workings part of the spreadsheet to accommodate the way that Excel calculates net present values:

- In cells B21, B22, B23 and B24 enter 0
- In cell A25 enter formula: =D9
- In cell B25 enter formula: =E9

Then put the following formula entry in E10: =NPV((B17/100),B21:B25).

Note: NPV stands for net present value.

***

The following five cells – E11, E12, E13, E14 and E15 – are not required to calculate the intrinsic value of the FTSE100 but they do provide useful information on the potential returns from investing in the FTSE100 – for basic rate and higher rate taxpayers.

These projected returns do not factor in the risk premium, which is only used to calculate the current fair market price (intrinsic value). If you want to factor in the risk premium, add: *100/(100+B15) to the formulae in E22 and E24. The higher rate tax calculations take into account the first tier of higher-rate tax, not the new super tier of higher-rate tax which was introduced for the 2010/2011 tax year.

These returns also do not take into account any Capital Gains Tax payable as there are shelters for investment which avoid Capital Gains Tax (see chapter 19) and, even without these shelters, any tax payable depends on individual circumstances – it is not possible to produce a universal forecast. If you want to take into account Capital Gains Tax as well, either separately or in addition to the risk premium, please see chapter 15.

E11: PROJECTED GROWTH FOR PERIOD % BR

This is the projected percentage total growth, for basic-rate taxpayers, of the end-period investment value on the initial investment, by expressing the change in investment value as a percentage of these original investment values (share price paid):

Formula entry in E11: =+(E9-B5)/B5*100

E12: PROJECTED ANNUAL GROWTH % BR

This converts the above overall projected growth from E11 to a compound annual percentage growth rate. This is the projected annual return from the investment. This information is very useful for comparing the projected annual return from this investment with the projected returns from alternative investments. To calculate this return you need to set up some formulae in the workings part of the spreadsheet:

- D21 title: Start investment value BR

- Formula entry in E21: =-B5 (negative B5)

- D22 title: End investment value BR

- Formula entry in E22: =E9

Then:

Formula entry in E12: =XIRR(E21:E22,E19:E20,.1)*100

XIRR is the Excel command which calculates a growth rate from a start and end investment value and a start and end investment date.

E13: END-PERIOD INVESTMENT VALUE HR

This is calculated by adding five years' worth of the average dividend, net of higher-rate tax, to the end-period FTSE100 price. Currently higher rate taxpayers suffer a further 25% tax deduction on the net dividend paid by the company. You would need to amend this formula if there were a change to this percentage higher-rate tax deduction.

To calculate this value, you need to set up some formulae in the workings part of the spreadsheet:

- **D23 Title**: Start investment value HR

- Formula entry in E23: = -B5 (i.e. negative)

- **D24 Title**: End Investment Value HR

- Formula entry in E24: =+E7*((1+(E8/100*0.75))^5)

Formula entry in E13: =E24

E14: PROJECTED TOTAL GROWTH % HR

This is the projected percentage total growth, for higher-rate taxpayers, of the end-period investment value on the initial investment:

Formula entry in E14: =(E13-B5)/B5*100

E15: PROJECTED ANNUAL GROWTH % HR

This converts the above overall projected growth from E14 to a compound annual percentage growth rate. This is the projected annual return from the investment for higher-rate taxpayers.

Formula entry in E15: =XIRR(E23:E24,E19:E20,.1)*100

***

E16: FTSE 100 INTRINSIC VALUE

This is the present discounted investment value BR (at the basic rate of tax), further discounted by the risk premium. This is the current intrinsic value of the FTSE100 calculated by the System from all the input values.

Formula entry in E16: =E10*100/(100+B15)

E17: VALUE AS % OF CURRENT PRICE

This expresses the current FTSE100 intrinsic value as a percentage of the current FTSE100 market price:

Formula entry in E17: =+E16/B5*100

THE FINAL VALUATION

After inputting all the formulae and the FTSE100 valuation data for 3 March 2009, your resulting spreadsheet should look like the sheet shown in Figure 7.3.

Figure 7.3 – FTSE100 valuation results

◇	A	B	C	D	E
1	**FTSE100 VALUATION**				
2	**INPUT DATA**			**RESULTS**	
3	Date	3-Mar-09		Current Net Dividend	209.0
4				Actual Dividend Growth % p.a.	-4.6
5	FTSE100 Price	3512.1		End-period Dividend	164.8
6				End-period Dividend Yield	3.3
7	FTSE100 Dividend Yield %	5.95		End-period FTSE100 Price	4951.7
8				Average Dividend Yield	4.6
9	Average Inflation Rate	1.5		End-period Investment Value BR	6212.0
10				Discounted Investment Value BR	5514.7
11	End-Period Inflation Rate	3.25		Projected growth for period % BR	76.9
12				Projected annual growth % BR	12.1
13	Real Dividend Growth Rate	-6.0		End-period Investment Value HR	5875.3
14				Projected growth for period % HR	67.3
15	Risk Premium%	10		Projected annual growth % HR	10.8
16				FTSE100 Intrinsic Value	**5013.3**
17	Redemption Yld % pa 5-yr Gilts	2.41		Value as % of Current Price	**142.7**
18	**WORKINGS**			**WORKINGS**	
19	Inflation Growth Factor	1.015		Start Date	01/01/00
20	Real Dividend Growth Factor	0.94		End Date	01/01/05
21		0		Start Investment Value BR	-3512.1
22		0		End Investment Value BR	6212.0
23		0		Start Investment Value HR	-3512.1
24		0		End Investment Value HR	5875.3
25	End-period Investment Value BR	6212.0		Real Dividend Start Period	-100.0
26				Real Dividend End Period	73.19
27				Real Dividend Growth Rate % p.a.	-6.0

As you can see, the intrinsic value of the FTSE100 as shown in E16 has been found to be 5013.3.

WHAT TO DO IF YOU DO NOT GET THE CORRECT RESULT

If you get a different result from an intrinsic value of 5013.3 in cell E16 when following this example, please check the data and formulae which you have input. There must be an error in one of these. To help you check the formulae I have provided them again in Figure 7.4.

To show the formulae in your own Excel spreadsheet hold down the 'Control' key and press the + and grave accent keys (`). You can use this command to toggle back and forth between the formulae display and the cell entry display.

In very rare combinations of operating systems and computer platforms it is possible that, even with the input values and formulae entered correctly, a different value from -6.0% may be calculated in cell E27, Real Dividend

Growth Rate % p.a. If this situation occurs, you should calculate the real dividend growth rate separately and enter the value directly into cell B13 using the following steps:

1. In cell A28 enter the title Real Dividend Growth Rate and in cell B28 enter an initial estimated value for the annual growth rate. A positive growth rate of, say, 2%, should be entered as 1.02 and a negative growth rate of, say, 2%, should be entered as 0.98 (i.e. 1 - 0.02).

2. In cell A29 enter the title Real Dividend Start Period and in cell B29 the value 100.

3. In cell A30 enter the title Real Dividend End Period and in cell B30 the formula: =B29*B28^5. This formula applies five years of the annual real dividend growth rate to the Real Dividend Start Period of 100.

4. By trial and error, adjust the Real Dividend Growth Rate in B28 until you get the value for the Real Dividend End Period, which you would have entered in cell E26 (in this case 73.19).

5. You will find that a value of 0.94, which equates to a negative annual growth rate of .06 (1-.94) p.a. or -6% p.a., produces a Real Dividend End Period in B30 of 73.39, very close to 73.19. Therefore enter -6 directly into B13. This should produce a FTSE100 intrinsic value very close to 5013.3 (any difference will be due to rounding).

6. Save the above labels and formulae in your master FTSE100 valuation spreadsheet and use the same methodology for future FTSE100 valuations to calculate the value for the Real Dividend Growth Rate to enter directly into cell B13. You should not rely on the annual growth figures calculated in cells E12 and E15. These are for information only and do not affect the calculation of the FTSE100 intrinsic value.

Figure 7.4 – FTSE100 valuation formulae

◇	A	B	D	E
1	**FTSE100 VALUATION**			
2	INPUT DATA		RESULTS	
3	Date	03-Mar-09	Current Net Dividend	=+B5*B7/100
4			Actual Dividend Growth % p.a.	=((B19*B20)-1)*100
5	FTSE100 Price	3512.1	End-period Dividend	=+E3*(1+(E4/100))^5
6			End-period Dividend Yield	=+(B11/10.5*3)+2.4
7	FTSE100 Dividend Yield %	5.95	End-period FTSE100 Price	=100/E6*E5
8			Average Dividend Yield	=+(B7+E6)/2
9	Average Inflation Rate	1.5	End-period Investment Value BR	=+E7*((1+(E8/100))^5)
10			Discounted Investment Value BR	=NPV((B17/100),B21:B25)
11	End-Period Inflation Rate	3.25	Projected growth for period % BR	=+(E9-B5)/B5*100
12			Projected annual growth % BR	=XIRR(E21:E22,E19:E20,0.1)*100
13	Real Dividend Growth Rate	=E27	End-period Investment Value HR	=E24
14			Projected growth for period % HR	=(E13-B5)/B5*100
15	Risk Premium%	10	Projected annual growth % HR	=XIRR(E23:E24,E19:E20,0.1)*100
16			FTSE100 Intrinsic Value	**=E10*100/(100+B15)**
17	Redemption Yld % pa 5-yr Gilts	2.41	Value as % of Current Price	=+E16/B5*100
18	WORKINGS		WORKINGS	
19	Inflation Growth Factor	=(1+(B9/100))	Start Date	36526
20	Real Dividend Growth Factor	=(1+(B13/100))	End Date	38353
21		0	Start Investment Value BR	=-B5
22		0	End Investment Value BR	=E9
23		0	Start Investment Value HR	=-B5
24		0	End Investment Value HR	=+E7*((1+(E8/100*0.75))^5)
25	End Period Investment Value BR	=E9	Real Dividend Start Period	-100
26			Real Dividend End Period	73.19
27			Real Dividend Growth Rate % p.a.	=XIRR(E25:E26,E19:E20,0.1)*100

Now that we have a valuation of the FTSE100, how should we interpret this?

INTERPRETING THE FINAL RESULT

This valuation calculated the intrinsic value of the FTSE100 on 3 March 2009 to be 5013.3. This was much higher than the market price of 3512.1. The valuation was 142.7% of the market price – a strong buy signal.

As is usual when panic sets in, the market had over-reacted and plunged below fair value. The valuation showed this over-reaction very clearly. In fact, it only took just over six months for the market to soar and reach the valuation produced by the System (14 September 2009). This surge represented a compound annual growth rate of 95%.

If you had been bold enough to take out a FTSE100 covered call warrant (of which more in chapter 17) on 3 March 2009, you could have more than quadrupled your investment in this short space of time. To put that growth into context, if you had invested in the median-performance professionally managed Equity fund over the ten years to end December 2010, your funds would have grown by only 49%, including reinvested dividends.

A major advantage of the System is that you can investigate the impact of other scenarios. Just change the relevant input values to see the impact of the changes on the overall valuation.

I have stress-tested this valuation for the FTSE100 on 3 March 2009 in chapter 16.

SETTING UP A MASTER VALUATION SHEET

When you are satisfied that you have input the formulae correctly, you should delete all the input data values, except the dates in cells E19 and E20, and save this spreadsheet as the master FTSE100 valuation tool under a file name of your choice.

Any subsequent valuations using this master spreadsheet should be saved under different file names to avoid the danger of new valuations being contaminated by data from previous valuations.

When you have constructed the master spreadsheet, you only need to enter the following data subsequently to obtain a FTSE100 valuation:

- Cell B3: Date of valuation (factual).

- Cell B5: FTSE100 price (factual).

- Cell B7: FTSE100 dividend yield (factual).

- Cell B9: Average inflation rate (factual).

- Cell B11: End-period inflation rate (factual).

- Cell B13 (direct input or calculated from E27): Real dividend growth rate (projected).

- Cell B15: Risk premium (projected but 10% is the default).

- Cell B17: Redemption yield % p.a. five-year gilts (factual).

THE NATURE OF THE INPUT DATA

By now it should be clear that the FTSE100 valuation system is based on first principles. It is not an irrational model built to fit past market movements as closely as possible. The system projects, using logical processes, how an investment in the FTSE100 today will build into an investment value in five years' time. That value is then discounted back to today's value, using well-established discounted cash-flow techniques which are frequently used to calculate the net present values of proposed investments.

However, whilst the System is entirely logical, could it fail through the garbage in/garbage out syndrome?

Let's look at the seven input values for the FTSE100 valuation system. Five are factual:

1. FTSE100 price.

2. FTSE100 dividend yield.

3. Average inflation rate.

4. End-period inflation rate.

5. Redemption yield on five-year gilts.

Two are judgemental:

6. Real dividend growth rate.

7. Risk premium.

It is worth looking more closely at the two judgemental inputs.

REAL DIVIDEND GROWTH RATE

This is the most potent input in the System. Historically the compound five-year real dividend growth rate has varied from 7.5% to -2.9% p.a. The long-term growth rate is just over 2% p.a. Normally it is appropriate to use 2.0% as a default value. The track record of two strategies using this approach is excellent, as has been seen in chapter 6.

However, you can use a different value if you believe that this is a more appropriate reflection of the UK's economic prospects – as I did above for the valuation of 3 March 2009. There I used a real growth rate of -6%; this was worse than experienced for any five-year period previously. Despite this, the valuation still showed that the FTSE100 price had fallen far too low, as was evidenced by the dramatic increase in the price over the following year.

RISK PREMIUM

The risk premium compensates for the higher risk of holding the FTSE100 compared with holding a virtually risk-free government bond to redemption.

This risk premium for the FTSE100 is lower than that for individual shares. This is because the risk is diluted through spreading the risk across a portfolio of 100 shares. Whilst a FTSE100 share can lose all or most of its value (remember Maxwell Communications?), the only circumstances in which all 100 shares in the FTSE100 would become valueless is through mass nationalisation without compensation or through a natural or man-made disaster affecting the whole UK.

Experience has shown that 10% is about the right risk premium for a five-year investment in the FTSE100 – but please note that this is not 10% per year: it is 10% for the whole five-year period. The risk premium does not need to be too high because, whilst there are downside risks, there is also upside potential. Furthermore, as explained in Part I, from the perspective of maintaining or increasing the real market value of your investments, holding cash or gilts is far from risk-free.

THE RELIABILITY OF THE SYSTEM'S FTSE 100 VALUATIONS

A good valuation system must not just be sound in theory, it must also work in practice. One way of assessing the reliability of the System's FTSE100 valuations is to examine the valuations before major turning points in the market. In the next chapter we shall also review the strong track record of the System's FTSE100 buy and sell signals since the start of the FTSE100 in 1984.

We shall look at the System valuations on 30 December 1999, the highest level ever reached by the FTSE100, and for 12 March 2003, which was the lowest level reached by the FTSE100 after the crash which followed the December 1999 peak.

Both these valuations used the default 2% p.a. for the real dividend growth rate. If there is no validity to the System, the valuations which it produces will bear no relation to the subsequent price performance. In fact, as you will see, the valuations have a strong correlation to subsequent price performance – not just in the direction but in the relative strength of the direction.

VALUATION FOR 30 DECEMBER 1999

Figure 7.5 – FTSE100 valuation for 30 December 1999

◇	A	B	C	D	E
1	**FTSE100 VALUATION**				
2	**INPUT DATA**			**RESULTS**	
3	Date	30-Dec-99		Current Net Dividend	141.4
4				Actual Dividend Growth % p.a.	5.8
5	FTSE100 Price	6930.2		End-period Dividend	187.6
6				End-period Dividend Yield	3.6
7	FTSE100 Dividend Yield %	2.04		End-period FTSE100 Price	5163.0
8				Average Dividend Yield	2.8
9	Average Inflation Rate	3.75		End-period Investment Value BR	5938.1
10				Discounted Investment Value BR	4418.5
11	End-Period Inflation Rate	4.32		Projected growth for period % BR	-14.3
12				Projected annual growth % BR	-3.0
13	Real Dividend Growth Rate	2.0		End-period Investment Value HR	5736.1
14				Projected growth for period % HR	-17.2
15	Risk Premium%	10		Projected annual growth % HR	-3.7
16				FTSE100 Intrinsic Value	**4016.8**
17	Redemption Yld % pa 5-yr Gilts	6.09		Value as % of Current Price	**58.0**
18	**WORKINGS**			**WORKINGS**	
19	Inflation Growth Factor	1.0375		Start Date	01/01/00
20	Real Dividend Growth Factor	1.02		End Date	01/01/05
21		0		Start Investment Value BR	-6930.2
22		0		End Investment Value BR	5938.1
23		0		Start Investment Value HR	-6930.2
24		0		End Investment Value HR	5736.1
25	End-period Investment Value BR	5938.1		Real Dividend Start Period	-100.0
26				Real Dividend End Period	
27				Real Dividend Growth Rate % p.a.	#NUM!

As you can see, this valuation, at the height of the dot.com mania, showed clearly the extent of the bubble which had formed. When the FTSE100 price was 6930.2, the valuation showed that the real value was only 4016.8, some 42% lower. The valuation was proved correct when the market immediately started crashing, reaching a low of 3287 on 12 March 2003 – a fall of 53% from the peak.

Another point to highlight is that the valuation projected the value of the FTSE100 at the end of 2004 to be 5163. The actual outcome was 4814, less than 7% different. Most professional analysts fail to predict the level of the FTSE100 one year ahead to that level of accuracy, let alone five years ahead.

VALUATION FOR 12 MARCH 2003

Figure 7.6 – FTSE100 Valuation for 12 March 2003

◇	A	B	C	D	E
1	**FTSE100 VALUATION**				
2	INPUT DATA			RESULTS	
3	Date	12-Mar-03		Current Net Dividend	139.4
4				Actual Dividend Growth % p.a.	4.5
5	FTSE100 Price	3287		End-period Dividend	173.9
6				End-period Dividend Yield	3.1
7	FTSE100 Dividend Yield %	4.24		End-period FTSE100 Price	5600.2
8				Average Dividend Yield	3.7
9	Average Inflation Rate	2.48		End-period Investment Value BR	6707.0
10				Discounted Investment Value BR	5611.8
11	End-Period Inflation Rate	2.47		Projected growth for period % BR	104.0
12				Projected annual growth % BR	15.3
13	Real Dividend Growth Rate	2.0		End-period Investment Value HR	6415.2
14				Projected growth for period % HR	95.2
15	Risk Premium%	10		Projected annual growth % HR	14.3
16				FTSE100 Intrinsic Value	**5101.6**
17	Redemption Yld % pa 5-yr Gilts	3.63		Value as % of Current Price	**155.2**
18	WORKINGS			WORKINGS	
19	Inflation Growth Factor	1.0248		Start Date	01/01/00
20	Real Dividend Growth Factor	1.02		End Date	01/01/05
21		0		Start Investment Value BR	-3287
22		0		End Investment Value BR	6707.0
23		0		Start Investment Value HR	-3287
24		0		End Investment Value HR	6415.2
25	End-period Investment Value BR	6707.0		Real Dividend Start Period	-100.0
26				Real Dividend End Period	
27				Real Dividend Growth Rate % p.a.	#NUM!

When the dot.com bubble burst the market over-reacted, as it always does when panic sets in. The FTSE100 reached a low of 3287 on 12 March 2003, well below the 4016.8 intrinsic value, which was calculated at the end of 1999.

At this low point, the System valued the FTSE100 at 5101.6, some 55% higher. This valuation was vindicated when the FTSE100 price subsequently soared, reaching 5102 on 23 June 2005, a compound annual capital growth rate of over 21%. It is also interesting to note that this valuation predicted the FTSE100 price at the end of the period, 12 March 2008, to be 5600. The actual outcome was 5776, only 3% different.

The valuation system therefore clearly does identify major market mispricing of the FTSE100 and highlights great profit opportunities, whether you are a bull or a bear.

8

USING THE SYSTEM'S MARKET VALUATIONS AS BUY AND SELL SIGNALS

The intrinsic valuations of the FTSE100 as a percentage of the market price can be used as buy and sell signals. The key question is: *What percentage valuation is a buy signal and what is a sell signal?*

Obviously the more extreme the underpricing or overpricing of the FTSE100, the stronger is the respective buy or sell signal. However, if you wait for a very strong signal, you will find very few buying or selling opportunities.

EXTREME SIGNALS

For example, you may set your sell signal at a 70% valuation. However, since 1984, using the 2% default for real dividend growth, you will only have found two sell signals. But on both occasions the subsequent fall in the market was very strong. The summary of these two sell signals is shown in Table 8.1.

Table 8.1 – Falls in FTSE100 prices after 70% valuations

Date	FTSE100 price	Value (%)	Date	FTSE100 price	Absolute fall in FTSE price (%)	Annualised fall (%)
8/10/87	2376	70	20/11/87	1633	30	95
11/5/98	6028	70	12/3/03	3287	46	12

The first of these two 70% valuations preceeded the infamous Black Monday Crash on 19 October 1987.

Whilst extreme signals, when they occur, are very valuable for investors in high-risk options or spread-bets, they do not occur frequently enough to form part of a long-term investment strategy.

THE OPTIMUM BUY AND SELL SIGNALS FOR THE FTSE 100

I have tested various buy/sell spreads to find the optimum balance between risk and investment frequency. My conclusion is that the optimum buy/sell spread for the FTSE100 (*but not for individual shares*) is 105/95, i.e. buy when the valuation first reaches 105% and subsequently sell when the valuation first falls to 95%. I have tested this spread for every trading day from the start of 1984 to the end of 2010 (i.e. a 27-year period).

For the 105/95 buy/sell spread I have calculated the capital growth of the FTSE100 for each buy/sell pair and for each sell/buy pair. I then calculated the cumulative capital growth for the times when the valuations indicated that you should be in the market and the times when the signals indicated that you should be out of the market.

The starting capital for both the period of FTSE100 investment and the period of FTSE100 disinvestment was a notional £100. A capital gain of 16.7% was made for the first period of FTSE100 investment, increasing the capital to £116.70. The next FTSE100 investment period produced a capital gain of 35.7%, thereby increasing the £116.70 to £158.40 and so on.

If the System's buy/sell signals work, the cumulative capital growth of the FTSE100 should be much higher when the signals indicated that you should be invested in the FTSE100 than when they indicated that you should be out of the market.

The results of these calculations are shown in Tables 8.2 and 8.3.

Table 8.2 – Performance of FTSE100 when buy signals indicated investment in the FTSE100 (105% to 95% spread)

Buy date	FTSE100 price	Sell date	FTSE100 price	Capital gain (%)	Years invested	Cumulative capital growth on £100 base
						100
26/06/1985	1236.5	21/11/1985	1443.1	16.7	0.41	117
28/10/1987	1658.4	11/07/1989	2250.9	35.8	1.7	158
09/04/1990	2227.7	24/12/1993	3412.3	53.2	3.71	243
07/03/1995	2977	12/10/1995	3523.8	18.4	0.6	287
11/07/2002	4230	23/01/2007	6227.6	47.2	4.54	423
16/08/2007	5859.9	05/10/2007	6595.8	12.6	0.14	476
				Total	11.1	
Cumulative capital gain (476 less 100)						376

Table 8.3 – Performance of FTSE100 when sell signals indicated disinvestment from the FTSE100 (105% to 95% spread)

Sell date	FTSE100 price	Buy date	FTSE100 price	Capital gain (loss) (%)	Years not invested	Cumulative capital growth on £100 base
						100
21/11/1985	1443.1	28/10/1987	1658.4	14.9	1.93	115
11/07/1989	2250.9	09/04/1990	2227.7	(-1)	0.75	114
24/12/1993	3412.3	07/03/1995	2977.0	(-12.8)	1.2	99
12/10/1995	3523.8	11/07/2002	4230.0	20	6.75	119
23/01/2007	6227.6	16/08/2007	5859.9	(-5.9)	0.56	112
05/10/2007	6595.8	19/11/2007	6120.8	(-7.2)	0.12	104
				Total	11.3	
Cumulative capital gain (104 less 100)						4

The results in Tables 8.2 and 8.3 were achieved using the default FTSE100 input values of 10% for risk premium and 2% p.a. for real dividend growth, together with the standard 105%/95% buy/sell spread. At the time of writing, there has been no sell signal subsequent to the buy signal on 19 November 2007.

All the other input data are the factual economic and market data for the valuation dates and can be verified. Even greater returns are possible by adjusting the input value for real dividend growth according to the prospects for corporate profitability over the prospective five-year investment period.

VALIDATION OF THE BUY AND SELL SIGNALS

The results of the validation tests are both startling and unequivocal:

- The cumulative capital gain on a £100 investment for the periods when the signals indicated that you should be invested in the FTSE100 was £376. This was **94 times** higher than the cumulative capital gain of just £4 for the periods when the signals indicated that you should not be invested in the FTSE100, even though the total time invested in the FTSE100, at 11.1 years, was less than the time not invested in the FTSE100, at 11.3 years.

- Over 11.3 years, the total cumulative capital gain of the FTSE100, for the periods when the signals indicated that you should not be invested in the FTSE100, was just 4%.

- The highest annualised capital gain of the FTSE100 non-invested periods, + 7.5%, was lower than the lowest capital gain of any of the FTSE100 invested periods (+8.9%).

- Furthermore, every buy signal has produced a capital gain upon the subsequent sell signal. In Part IV, I will explain two FTSE100 investment strategies which use these valuation signals – with great success to date. One of these strategies is lower risk than remaining fully invested in the FTSE100 at all times because cash investment is used when the signals indicate that the FTSE100 offers poor value.

I believe that the probability of these outstanding results occurring by chance is infinitesimally small.

MARKET TOPS AND BOTTOMS

It is important to stress that the buy and sell signals will rarely coincide with the precise bottoms and tops of the market. This is because falling prices tend to fall too low because of panic/fear and rising prices tend to rise too far because of greed/over-exuberance. However, by buying near the bottom and selling near the top you should achieve much higher investment returns than remaining permanently passively invested.

If you become expert with moving averages (see pages 195 to 196, chapter 17) you could use moving average trends in combination with my System's buy and sell signals to try to get as close to the bottoms and tops of the market as possible.

THE IMPORTANCE OF THE FTSE 100 DIVIDEND

Eagle-eyed readers will have spotted from the above table that there was a buy signal on 19 November 2007, when the FTSE100 stood at 6120.8. Using the 2% default for real dividend growth, there has been no subsequent sell signal. However, under the weight of the credit crunch, the FTSE100 price collapsed during 2008 and the early part of 2009. Does this false buy signal show that the System does not work?

On the contrary, I would argue that this is the exception which proves the rule. It shows that the default real dividend growth rate of 2% for the next five years was not appropriate for November 2007. Some astute commentators and fund managers saw the credit crunch coming. Jeff Randall had been warning in his *Daily Telegraph* column that the credit bubble was going to burst and end in tears. Similarly Neil Woodford of Invesco had spotted the danger signals in banks and, before the credit crunch, had stripped bank shares from his flagship High Income fund despite the banks (then!) paying high dividends.

In the three years from 19 November 2007 to 19 November 2010, the FTSE100 dividend fell by 13% from 203.2 to 176.6. Assuming that the dividend then stabilised and increased in line with the projected average inflation rate of 2.88% p.a. (but with no real increase), the actual dividend at the end of the five-year period in November 2012 would be 186.9 (176.6 x 1.0288^2). Discounted back by the average inflation rate for five years to the real November 2007 value, this end-period dividend would be worth just 162.2: 186.9 x (100/102.88)^5.

Inputting 203.2 as the value for Real Dividend Start Period and 162.2 as the value for Real Dividend End Period produces a compound real dividend growth rate of -4.4% p.a. (negative). Changing the real dividend growth rate from 2% real to -4.4% real for the valuation of 19 November 2007 produces a valuation of 78.7%, as shown in Figure 8.1. Far from being a buy signal, this is a strong sell signal.

So there is nothing wrong with the System. Those who had foreseen the forthcoming collapse in the FTSE100 dividend would, with the System, have successfully been able to predict the collapse in the FTSE100 price by inputting a negative real dividend growth rate instead of the default positive 2% p.a. Yet again we see how important the dividend is to the FTSE100 price.

You should therefore be prepared to reduce substantially the FTSE100 default dividend growth rate if you see corporate earnings (on which dividends depend) collapsing, with no sign of an early change in the wider economic conditions.

Figure 8.1 – Valuation of FTSE100 on 19 November 2007. The real dividend growth rate reflects the impending collapse in the FTSE100 dividend.

◇	A	B	C	D	E
1	**FTSE100 VALUATION**				
2	**INPUT DATA**			**RESULTS**	
3	Date	19-Nov-07		Current Net Dividend	203.2
4				Actual Dividend Growth % p.a.	-1.7
5	FTSE100 Price	6120.8		End-period Dividend	187.0
6				End-period Dividend Yield	3.3
7	FTSE100 Dividend Yield %	3.32		End-period FTSE100 Price	5627.3
8				Average Dividend Yield	3.3
9	Average Inflation Rate	2.88		End-period Investment Value BR	6626.0
10				Discounted Investment Value BR	5296.8
11	End-Period Inflation Rate	3.23		Projected growth for period % BR	8.3
12				Projected annual growth % BR	1.6
13	Real Dividend Growth Rate	-4.4		End-period Investment Value HR	6364.0
14				Projected growth for period % HR	4.0
15	Risk Premium%	10		Projected annual growth % HR	0.8
16				**FTSE100 Intrinsic Value**	**4815.2**
17	Redemption Yld % pa 5-yr Gilts	4.58		**Value as % of Current Price**	**78.7**
18	**WORKINGS**			**WORKINGS**	
19	Inflation Growth Factor	1.0288		Start Date	01/01/00
20	Real Dividend Growth Factor	0.96		End Date	01/01/05
21		0		Start Investment Value BR	-6120.8
22		0		End Investment Value BR	6626.0
23		0		Start Investment Value HR	-6120.8
24		0		End Investment Value HR	6364.0
25	End-period Investment Value BR	6626.0		Real Dividend Start Period	-203.2
26				Real Dividend End Period	162.2
27				Real Dividend Growth Rate % p.a.	-4.4

9

A STEP-BY-STEP GUIDE TO VALUING INDIVIDUAL SHARES

In this chapter I will take you through, step-by-step, how to create a spreadsheet to calculate the intrinsic value of individual shares.

A MORE DIFFICULT TASK THAN VALUING THE MARKET

The first thing to say is that it is much more difficult to value an individual share than it is to value an index such as the FTSE100. The logical valuation structure is the same as that of the FTSE100 valuation system but there are three judgement-based input values instead of two and it is more difficult to assess these input values. These three judgement-based inputs are:

- **Risk premium**: There is no default risk premium, as there is for the FTSE100, and the range of risk premiums can vary widely from share to share.

- **End-period dividend yield**: Whereas we could determine an appropriate end-period dividend yield for the FTSE100 by reference to the projected end-period inflation rate, this is only one of the factors involved in determining the end-period dividend yield for an individual share. I will explain the process required.

- **Real dividend growth**: We have seen in chapter 7 that the default assumption of a 2% dividend growth rate is *not always* appropriate for a FTSE100 valuation. For an individual share, a default assumption is *never* appropriate. I will go through the steps required to determine this value.

You should also note that the System is not suitable for valuing collective investments such as investment or unit trusts.

INPUT DATA

If you are using Microsoft Excel, ensure, via the Tools/Add-ons menu, that the box for the Analysis Toolpak is checked.

SETTING UP THE SPREADSHEET

Set column widths as follows:

Column	Width
A	30
B	16
C	2
D	27
E	9

You should also set the number format for each data cell, except date fields, to *number* and set the number of decimal places for displaying each number to 1 or 2.

ENTER INPUT FIELD TITLES INTO COLUMN A

Although several of the input data fields are the same as for the FTSE100 valuation, for convenient reference I will repeat these steps here. I will use, as an example, the data to value International Power on 16 October 2009.

This example uses, amongst other elements, consensus broker forecasts from Digital Look (**www.digitallook.com**). The Digital Look service is free but you have to register for it.

You can, of course, use your own forecasts instead; indeed, if consensus broker forecasts are not available for the share which you wish to value, you *must* use your own forecasts.

To start, you need to enter the labels of the input fields in column A. These are:

- date
- share name or ID
- share price
- share net dividend yield %

- target dividend cover

- actual end-period dividend cover

- average inflation rate

- end-period inflation rate

- real dividend growth rate

- default real dividend growth rate

- risk premium %

- redemption yield % p.a. five-year gilts.

Your spreadsheet will then look like the one shown in Figure 9.1.

Figure 9.1 – Input field labels for the share valuation spreadsheet

◇	A	B	C	D	E
1	**SHARE VALUATION**				
2	INPUT DATA			RESULTS	
3	Date				
4	Share Name or ID				
5	Share Price				
6	Share Net Dividend Yield %				
7	Target Dividend Cover				
8	Actual End-Period Dividend Cover				
9	Average Inflation Rate				
10	End-Period Inflation Rate				
11	Real Dividend Growth Rate				
12	Default Real Dividend Growth Rate				
13	Risk Premium %				
14	Redemption Yld % pa 5-yr Gilts				
15	**WORKINGS**				
16					
17					
18				WORKINGS	
19					
20					
21					
22					
23					
24					
25					
26					
27					
28					

You then need to enter the input data for each of these fields in column B.

ENTER INPUT DATA INTO COLUMN B

CELL B3: DATE

Enter the date of the data from which you are making the valuation.

Entry in B3: 16/10/09

CELL B4: SHARE NAME OR ID

Enter the name or ID of the share.

Entry in B4: International Power

CELL B5: SHARE PRICE

You can obtain the price of individual shares from the Digital Look website (**companyresearch.digitallook.com/cgi-bin/dlmedia/investing/screening_tools/performance_tables**).

Click on the index of which the company forms part (e.g. FTSE100, FTSE250, FTSE AIM, etc.) and choose the 'Overview' table.

Scroll down to the company name and you will see the share price. If you are not sure of the index in which your share is listed, choose the FTSE All-Share performance table.

For our example, International Power was priced at 264.5 on 16/10/09.

Entry in B5: 264.5

CELL B6: SHARE NET DIVIDEND YIELD %

To obtain the dividend yield, the process is the same as for finding the share's price – on the Overview table on Digital Look read across to the column headed 'Div Yield'.

The share net dividend yield is the net dividend for the last financial year (including any final dividend declared but not yet paid) expressed as a percentage of the current share price.

Dividend yields quoted in the *Financial Times* may vary slightly to those given by Digital Look as the *FT*'s yield figures include any changes from interim dividends paid after the final dividend (companies generally pay two dividends per year – a smaller interim and a larger final dividend when the full results for the year are known).

Entry in B6: 4.59

CELL B7: TARGET DIVIDEND COVER

As discussed in Part II, the dividend cover informs the investor how sustainable dividend payments are. A company which is paying out nearly all its earnings as a dividend is likely to reduce its dividend in the future unless earnings rise substantially. To recap, the dividend cover is calculated by dividing the earnings per share by the dividend per share.

A dividend cover of 2 is usually regarded as secure, although I normally use a dividend cover target of 2.25 as a safety margin. The target dividend cover is used in the calculation of the projected end-period share price.

Entry in B7: 2.25

CELL B8: ACTUAL END-PERIOD DIVIDEND COVER

This is the forecast actual end-period dividend cover, which forms part of the calculation of the critical end-period dividend yield.

This figure can be obtained through Digital Look. At first follow the steps stated above for finding out the share price.

Then, click on the name of the company you are valuing. In this example this is International Power. Scroll down to the 'Forecasts' section and note both the EPS (earnings per share) and Div. (dividend per share) forecasts for the final year of the forecast.

Then divide the earnings per share by the dividend per share to get the final year forecast for the dividend cover. Use this as the figure for the end-period dividend cover, unless you believe that this cover will change by the end of the five-year period in which case you should use the changed cover instead.

In this example, there are three years of forecast figures available. The third-year forecast for EPS is 35.78p and the third year forecast for Div. is 14.63 and so the forecast dividend cover is:

```
35.78/14.63 = 2.45
```

Entry in B8: 2.45

CELL B9: AVERAGE INFLATION RATE

You can obtain the average inflation rate from the Bank of England website (**www.bankofengland.co.uk/statistics/yieldcurve**).

The Bank of England produces daily reports to show inflation expectations as implied by the prices of market instruments. Scroll down to the section headed 'Implied Inflation (Government Liability)' against an Excel icon.

Click on this wording and a dialogue box will appear. Click on OK to open the file (normally with Microsoft Excel). The file should download and appear on-screen.

Click on the 'spot curve' tab and scroll sideways to the column headed 5.00. This shows the average inflation expected over the next five years. Read across from the required date on the left (normally the last date if you are doing a current valuation) to get the appropriate figure under the column headed 5.00.

Normally there is a time-lag of one working day in this data being updated. Don't worry if you have to use the previous day's figure as there is normally very little change in the figure over one day.

I do not advise using the System if either the average or end-period inflation rate is over 10.5%. In the case of this example, the figure shown is 2.39%.

Entry in B9: 2.39

CELL B10: END-PERIOD INFLATION RATE

The source for the end-period inflation rate is the same as above for the average inflation rate.

Click on the 'fwd curve' tab and scroll sideways to the column headed 5.00. This shows the inflation rate expected at the end of the next five years. Read across from the required date on the left (normally the last date if you are doing a current valuation) to get the appropriate figure under the column headed 5.00.

Normally there is a time-lag of one working day in this data being updated. Don't worry if you have to use the previous day's figure as there is normally very little change in the figure over one day.

In our example, the figure shown in the spreadsheet is 3.17%.

Entry in B10: 3.17

CELL B11: REAL DIVIDEND GROWTH RATE

This is the real compound growth rate percentage p.a. expected in the dividend over the next five years. To calculate this key input, there are eleven steps you have to follow.

Some of these steps will involve making entries into the workings part of the spreadsheet (column A for field titles and column B for the data or formulae). The source for the data is the Digital Look forecast data that was referenced above.

With columns D and E, column D will be comprised of the field titles and column E holds the data or formulae.

Step 1. Cells D3 and E3: Current net dividend

You should first enter the formula to calculate the **current net dividend into cell E3**.

Formula in E3: =+B5*B6/100

Step 2. Cells A22 and B22: Last forecast year dividend per share

This is the final forecast year dividend per share and is the same dividend per share figure used in the calculation of the end-period dividend cover (B8).

Entry in B22: 14.63

Step 3. Cells A23 and B23: No. of years not forecast

Enter the number of years for which no forecast is available. As, in this example, we have a third year forecast (sometimes only two forecast years are available) there are two years for which a forecast is not available.

Entry in B23: 2

Step 4. Cells A12 and B12: Default real dividend growth rate

This is the real dividend growth rate percentage which is used for the final years of the forecast in the absence of broker forecast figures. Use your judgement about the company and the economic backdrop to determine this figure, or just use the same figure which you would use for a FTSE100 valuation.

Entry in B12: 1

Step 5. Cells A24 and B24: Default actual dividend growth factor

This is calculated from the default real dividend growth rate and the average inflation rate.

Formula entry in B24: =(1+(B12/100))*(1+(B9/100))

Step 6. Cells A25 and B25: Current net dividend

This is the negative of the current net dividend, which is calculated in Cell E3 of the spreadsheet.

Formula entry in B25: =-E3

Step 7. Cells A26 and B26: End-period dividend

This is calculated from the final forecast year dividend, compounded by the default actual dividend growth rate for the remaining years for which there is no consensus broker forecast.

Formula entry in B26: =+B22*B24^B23

Step 8. Cells D19 and E19: Start date

Choose a date at the beginning of a year. Ensure that E19 is set to date format.

Data entry in E19: 01/01/00

Step 9. Cells D20 and E20: End date

Choose a date five years later than the date in E19. Ensure that E20 is set to date format.

Data entry in E20: 01/01/05

Step 10. Cells A27 and B27: Actual dividend growth rate

This is the compound actual dividend growth rate over the five-year period, given the current dividend and the projected end-period dividend.

Formula entry in B27: =XIRR(B25:B26,E19:E20,0.1)*100

And finally:

Step 11. Cells A28 and B28: Real dividend growth rate

This is calculated from the above actual dividend growth rate and the average inflation rate.

Formula entry in B28: =(100+B27)/(100+B9)*100-100

Then:

Formula entry in B11: =B28

You can, of course, use your own assumption for the real dividend growth rate rather than use the growth rate implied by the consensus broker forecasts. If so, just enter this figure directly in B11 but ensure that the dates are completed in cells E19 and E20.

CELL B13: RISK PREMIUM %

There is no agreed method for determining the risk premium of a share.

As with the FTSE100, the risk premium compensates for the greater risk of holding shares than a virtually risk-free gilt. In the case of the FTSE100, the default risk premium is 10% for the five-year investment period.

In the case of a share, the minimum risk premium is higher, at 15%, because there is less risk in the FTSE100 due to the diversification of investment over 100 shares. However, the risk premium of a specific share could be considerably higher. In the System the end-period investment value is risk-adjusted as follows:

```
end-period investment value x 100/(100 + risk
premium)
```

It is worth discussing what risk is being covered.

What risk is covered within the risk premium?

Compared with buying a gilt and locking into a fixed yield, if held to redemption, you suffer the following main risks when buying a share:

- The expected dividends and the associate dividend cover may turn out lower than projected.

- In a worst case, the company could go bust.

- Interest rates and/or inflation may increase, thereby reducing the relative attractions of holding shares versus holding cash.

Calculating risk premium using share price volatility

Normally company risk premiums are calculated with reference to the volatility of the share price. ShareMaestro currently uses a measure called beta, which measures the relative volatility of the share price to the volatility of the market. The beta of a share is available from Digital Look.

The default ShareMaestro method is to set a risk premium of 15% if beta is 1 or below. If beta is above 1, multiply it by 100, deduct 100, halve the result and add this to 15 to get the risk premium.

So, in this case, where the beta value is 1.11, the risk premium is:

```
15 + (.5 x ((1.11 x 100)-100)) = 15 + 5.5 = 20.5
```

If the resulting risk premium comes to more than 75 (which will be very rare), cap it at 75.

However, there is a strong case that volatility of earnings is much more of a risk factor than the volatility of the share price. An alternative method to calculate the risk premium according to past volatility of earnings is as follows.

Calculating risk premium using earnings volatility

- Look at the earnings per share (EPS) figures for the past five years using Digital Look. If there has been a steady increase in EPS for every year, use 15% as the risk premium.

- If there has been a decline in any year, find the biggest absolute fall over the period between one year and any subsequent year.

- Measure the percentage fall from the top to the bottom.

- Add this percentage fall to the 15% minimum risk premium up to a maximum of 75 to calculate the risk premium; the maximum risk premium is 75%.

Example

For share X, the biggest drop in EPS over the last five years was from 60 in Year 2 to 48 in Year 4. The represents a 20% drop (12/60 x 100). Therefore, add 20 to 15 to make a risk premium of 35%. If the drop had been 70%, the overall risk premium would be capped at 75%.

Think about the future prospects of the company

Ultimately you need to review any formulaic risk premium with your own judgement about the future prospects of the company. Essentially the risk premium is a confidence limit on the projected sustainable dividend stream of the company. For this reason cyclical companies, such as house-builders, tend to attract high risk premiums, whereas companies with more stable and predictable dividend streams, such as supermarket groups, tend to attract low risk premiums.

In the case of International Power, there has been a steady increase in EPS over the last five years. The risk premium is therefore 15%.

Formula entry in cell B13: 15

CELL B14: REDEMPTION YIELD % P.A. FIVE-YEAR GILTS

You can obtain the redemption yield per year for five-year gilts from the *Financial Times* (at: **markets.ft.com/research/Markets/Data-Archive**).

Scroll down to the bottom of the page and, in the drop-down menus, select:

Category: Bonds and Rates

Report: FTSE UK Gilts Indices

Date: Select the date of your choice (in this case 16 March 2009) and click on the 'download' button and the report should appear as a PDF.

In the middle of the page, there are three rows under the heading 'Yield Indices'. Select the first row '5 yrs' and the value for the appropriate date. This is the compound risk-free interest rate for a gilt held for five years to redemption. For this example the figure shown is 2.66, so we enter this in B14.

Entry in B14: 2.66

RESULTS

ENTER RESULTS FIELD TITLES INTO COLUMN D

Having completed the input data, you need to enter the labels of the results fields into column D. These are:

- current net dividend
- actual divided growth % p.a.
- end-period dividend
- end-period dividend yield
- end-period share price
- average dividend yield
- end-period investment value BR (BR = taking account of basic rate tax)
- discounted investment value BR
- projected growth for perod % BR
- projected annual growth % BR
- end-period investment value HR (HR = taking account of higher rate tax)
- projected growth for period % HR
- projected annual growth % HR
- share intrinsic value
- value as a perentage of current price.

You should also enter the labels for the cells that contain the rest of the associated workings. Your spreadsheet will then look like the one shown in Figure 9.2.

Figure 9.2 – Result field labels for the share valuation spreadsheet

◇	A	B	C	D	E
1	**SHARE VALUATION**				
2	INPUT DATA			RESULTS	
3	Date	16-Oct-09		Current Net Dividend	12.1
4	Share Name or ID	International Power		Actual Dividend Growth % p.a.	
5	Share Price	264.5		End-Period Dividend	
6	Share Net Dividend Yield %	4.59		End-Period Dividend Yield	
7	Target Dividend Cover	2.25		End-Period Share Price	
8	Actual End-Period Dividend Cover	2.45		Average Dividend Yield	
9	Average Inflation Rate	2.39		End-period Investment Value BR	
10	End-Period Inflation Rate	3.17		Discounted Investment Value BR	
11	Real Dividend Growth Rate	2.74		Projected growth for period % BR	
12	Default Real Dividend Growth Rate	1.00		Projected annual growth % BR	
13	Risk Premium %	15		End-period Investment Value HR	
14	Redemption Yld % pa 5-yr Gilts	2.66		Projected growth for period % HR	
15	**WORKINGS**			Projected annual growth % HR	
16		0		Share Intrinsic Value	
17		0		Value as % of Current Price	
18		0		**WORKINGS**	
19		0		Start Date	01/01/00
20	End-Period Investment Value BR	0.0		End Date	01/01/05
21	End-Period FTSE100 yield %	3.3		Start Investment Value BR	
22	Last forecast year dividend per share	14.63		End Investment Value BR	
23	No. of years not forecast	2		Start Investment Value HR	
24	Default actual dividend growth factor	1.0341		End Investment Value HR	
25	Current Net Dividend	-12.1			
26	End-period dividend	15.6			
27	Actual dividend growth rate	5.20			
28	Real dividend growth rate	2.74			

Let's look now at how to populate these results fields. I describe each results field and the formula which you should enter to calculate the relevant figure for the field.

ENTER RESULTS FORMULAE INTO COLUMN E

CELL E4: ACTUAL DIVIDEND GROWTH % P.A.

Formula entry in E4: =(100+B11)*(1+(B9/100))-100

CELL E5: END-PERIOD DIVIDEND

Formula entry in E5: =+E3*(1+(E4/100))^5

CELL E6: END-PERIOD DIVIDEND YIELD

To calculate this value, you first need to calculate the end-period FTSE100 yield. This is the projected FTSE100 dividend yield at the end of the five-year period. It takes into account the projected inflation rate for the end of the period.

The calculations for this yield in ShareMaestro are proprietary and complex. The following formula uses the projected end-period inflation rate and produces a similar result to the one produced by ShareMaestro.

Entry in cell A21: End-period FTSE100 yield %

Formula entry in B21: =+(B10/10.5*3)+2.4

This formula might need to be altered if the tax treatment of dividends for basic-rate taxpayers were changed. Since 1997, the dividends actually paid to shareholders by companies are deemed to be net of the basic rate of personal Income Tax.

The end-period share dividend yield is then calculated by adjusting the end-period FTSE100 dividend yield in accordance with the ratio of the target dividend cover to the projected actual end-period dividend cover for the share.

This calculation assumes that by the end of the five-year period the share's future sustainable growth will be in line with that of the FTSE100. However, as well as dividend cover, a share's prospective long-term sustainable dividend growth will influence the dividend yield. The market will accept a relatively low current dividend yield if it expects the dividend to increase strongly. Conversely, the market will require a higher current dividend yield if it expects the dividend to remain static or to fall.

You can adjust the end-period dividend yield by adjusting the target dividend cover. Consequently, if you expect the share's dividend growth to significantly exceed that of the market in Years 5 to 10, you should reduce the target dividend cover (B7) accordingly. Conversely, if you expect the share's dividend growth to fall significantly short of the market in Years 5 to 10, you should increase the target dividend cover (B7) accordingly.

For example, if you expect that, at the end of the five-year period, the share's dividend growth (with dividend cover remaining unchanged) would be so strong as to produce double the dividend at the end of the next five years than if it merely matched the FTSE100 dividend growth, you would halve the target dividend cover input in B7.

The end-period share dividend yield (E6) is calculated by multiplying the end-period FTSE100 dividend yield (B21) by the target dividend cover (B7) divided by the projected end-period share dividend cover (B8).

Formula entry in E6: =B21*B7/B8

CELL E7: END-PERIOD SHARE PRICE

This price follows directly from the end-period dividend and the end-period dividend yield. It is calculated as follows:

Formula entry in E7: =100/E6*E5

CELL E8: AVERAGE DIVIDEND YIELD

This is calculated from the average of the current dividend yield and the end-period dividend yield:

Formula entry in E8: =+(B6+E6)/2

CELL E9: END-PERIOD INVESTMENT VALUE BR

This is the projected end-period investment value for basic-rate taxpayers (BR). It takes no account of any potential Capital Gains Tax. This value is calculated by adding to the end-period share price five years' worth of the average dividend, net of basic rate tax (i.e. the net dividend paid by the company):

Formula entry in E9: =+E7*((1+(E8/100))^5)

CELL E10: DISCOUNTED INVESTMENT VALUE BR

This value is calculated by discounting the above projected BR investment value (in five year's time) back to today's value by using, as a discount rate, the gross annual yield on five-year gilt held in redemption.

To calculate the discounted present value of the end-period investment value, you need to set up some formulae in the workings part of the spreadsheet:

- In cells B16, B17, B18 and B19 enter 0.

- In A20 insert the title: End-Period Investment Value BR

- In cell B20 enter the formula: =E9

Then put the following formula entry in E10: =NPV((B14/100),B16:B20)

Note: NPV stands for net present value.

***

The following five cells – E11, E12, E13, E14 and E15 – are not required to calculate the intrinsic value of the share but they do provide useful information on the potential returns from investing in the share for basic rate and higher rate taxpayers.

These projected returns do not factor in the risk premium, which is only used to calculate the current fair market price (intrinsic value). If you want to factor in the risk premium, add *100/(100+B13) to the formulae in E22 and E24.

The higher rate tax calculations take into account the first tier of higher-rate tax, not the new super tier of higher-rate tax which was introduced for the 2010/2011 tax year. These returns also do not take into account any Capital Gains Tax payable as there are shelters for investment which avoid Capital Gains Tax (see chapter 19) and, even without these shelters, any tax payable depends on individual circumstances. If you want to take into account Capital Gains Tax as well, either separately or in addition to the risk premium, please see chapter 15.

E11: PROJECTED GROWTH FOR PERIOD % BR

This is the total projected percentage growth, for basic-rate taxpayers, of the end-period investment value on the current share price:

Formula entry in E11: =+(E9-B5)/B5*100

E12: PROJECTED ANNUAL GROWTH % BR

This converts the overall projected growth from E11 to a compound annual percentage growth. This is the projected annual return from the investment. To do this you need to set up some formulae in the workings part of the spreadsheet:

- D21 Title: 'Start Investment Value BR'
- Formula entry in E21: = -B5 (i.e. negative)
- D22 Title: 'End Investment Value BR'
- Formula entry in E22: =E9

Then:

Formula entry in E12: =XIRR(E21:E22,E19:E20,.1)*100

E13: END-PERIOD INVESTMENT VALUE HR

This is the projected end-period investment value for higher-rate taxpayers (HR). It takes no account of any potential Capital Gains Tax. This is calculated by adding to the end-period share price five years' worth of the average dividend, net of higher rate tax. Currently higher-rate taxpayers suffer a further 25% tax deduction on the net dividend paid by the company.

To calculate this value, you need to set up some formulae in the workings part of the spreadsheet:

- D23 title: Start investment value HR

- Formula entry in E23: = -B5 (i.e. negative)

- D24 title: End investment value HR

- Formula entry in E24: =+E7*((1+(E8/100*0.75))^5)

Formula entry in E13: =E24

E14: PROJECTED GROWTH FOR PERIOD % HR

This is the projected percentage total growth, for higher-rate taxpayers, of the end-period investment value on the current share price:

Formula entry in E14: =(E13-B5)/B5*100

E15: PROJECTED ANNUAL GROWTH % HR

This converts the above overall projected growth from E14 to a compound annual percentage growth. This is the projected annual return from the investment for higher-rate taxpayers.

Formula entry in E15: =XIRR(E23:E24,E19:E20,.1)*100

***

E16: SHARE INTRINSIC VALUE

This is the present discounted investment value BR (at the basic rate of tax), further discounted by the risk premium.

Formula entry in E16: =E10*100/(100+B13)

E17: VALUE AS % OF CURRENT PRICE

This expresses the current share intrinsic value as a percentage of the current share market price:

Formula entry in E17: =+E16/B5*100

THE FINAL VALUATION

After inputting all the formulae and the International Power valuation data for 16 October 2009, your resulting spreadsheet should look like the sheet shown in Figure 9.3.

Figure 9.3 – Results of valuing International Power on 16/10/09

◇	A	B	C	D	E
1	**SHARE VALUATION**				
2	INPUT DATA			RESULTS	
3	Date	16-Oct-09		Current Net Dividend	12.1
4	Share Name or ID	International Power		Actual Dividend Growth % p.a.	5.2
5	Share Price	264.5		End-Period Dividend	15.6
6	Share Net Dividend Yield %	4.59		End-Period Dividend Yield	3.04
7	Target Dividend Cover	2.25		End-Period Share Price	515.2
8	Actual End-Period Dividend Cover	2.45		Average Dividend Yield	3.81
9	Average Inflation Rate	2.39		End-period Investment Value BR	621.2
10	End-Period Inflation Rate	3.17		Discounted Investment Value BR	544.8
11	Real Dividend Growth Rate	2.74		Projected growth for period % BR	134.9
12	Default Real Dividend Growth Rate	1.00		Projected annual growth % BR	18.6
13	Risk Premium %	15		End-period Investment Value HR	593.2
14	Redemption Yld % pa 5-yr Gilts	2.66		Projected growth for period % HR	124.3
15	WORKINGS			Projected annual growth % HR	17.5
16		0		**Share Intrinsic Value**	**473.8**
17		0		**Value as % of Current Price**	**179.1**
18		0		WORKINGS	
19		0		Start Date	01/01/00
20	End-Period Investment Value BR	621.2		End Date	01/01/05
21	End-Period FTSE100 yield %	3.3		Start Investment Value BR	-264.5
22	Last forecast year dividend per share	14.63		End Investment Value BR	621.2
23	No. of years not forecast	2		Start Investment Value HR	-264.5
24	Default actual dividend growth factor	1.0341		End Investment Value HR	593.2
25	Current Net Dividend	-12.1			
26	End-period dividend	15.6			
27	Actual dividend growth rate	5.20			
28	Real dividend growth rate	2.74			

As you can see, the intrinsic value of the FTSE100 as shown in E16 has been found to be 473.8.

WHAT TO DO IF YOU DO NOT GET THE CORRECT RESULT

If you get a different result from an intrinsic value of 473.8 in cell E16 when following this example, please check the data and formulae which you have input. There must be an error in one of these. To help you check the formulae I have provided them again in Figure 9.4.

To show the formulae in your own Excel spreadsheet hold down the 'Control' key and press the + and grave accent keys (`). You can use this command to toggle back and forth between the formulae display and the cell entry display.

In very rare combinations of operating systems and computer platforms it is possible that, even with the input values and formulae entered correctly, a different value from 5.2 may be calculated in cell B27, Actual dividend growth rate. If this situation occurs, you should calculate the actual dividend growth rate separately and enter the value directly into cell B27 using the following steps:

1. In cell A29 enter the title Actual Dividend Growth Rate and in cell B29 enter an initial estimated value for the annual growth rate. A positive growth rate of, say 2%, should be entered as 1.02 and a negative growth rate of, say 2%, should be entered as 0.98 (i.e. 1 - 0.02).

2. In cell A30 enter the title Actual Dividend Start Period and in cell B30 the formula: =E3. The value in this case is 12.1.

3. In cell A31 enter the title Actual Dividend End Period and in cell B31 the formula: =B30*B29^5. This formula applies five years of the annual growth rate to the Actual Dividend Start Period of 12.1.

4. By trial and error, adjust the Actual Dividend Growth Rate in B29 until you get the same value for the End period dividend as calculated in cell B26 (in this case 15.6).

5. You will find that a value of 1.052, which equates to a annual growth rate of 5.2%, produces an end period dividend in B31 of 15.64, very close to 15.6. Therefore enter 5.2 directly into B27. This should produce a share intrinsic value very close to 473.8.

6. Save the above labels and formulae in your master share valuation spreadsheet and use the same methodology for future share valuations to calculate the value for the Actual dividend growth rate to enter directly into cell B27. You should not rely on the annual growth figures calculated in cells E12 and E15; these are for information only and do not affect the calculation of the share intrinsic value.

Figure 9.4 – Share valuation spreadsheet formulae

	A	B	C	D	E
1	**SHARE VALUATION**				
2	INPUT DATA			RESULTS	
3	Date	16-Oct-09		Current Net Dividend	=+B5*B6/100
4	Share Name or ID	International Power		Actual Dividend Growth % p.a.	=(100+B11)*(1+(B9/100))-100
5	Share Price	264.5		End-Period Dividend	=E3*(1+(E4/100))^5
6	Share Net Dividend Yield %	4.59		End-Period Dividend Yield	=B21*B7/B8
7	Target Dividend Cover	2.25		End-Period Share Price	=100/E6*E5
8	Actual End-Period Dividend Cover	2.45		Average Dividend Yield	=+(B6+E6)/2
9	Average Inflation Rate	2.39		End-period Investment Value BR	=+E7*((1+(E8/100))^5)
10	End-Period Inflation Rate	3.17		Discounted Investment Value BR	=NPV((B14/100),B16:B20)
11	Real Dividend Growth Rate	=B28		Projected growth for period % BR	=+(E9-B5)/B5*100
12	Default Real Dividend Growth Rate	1		Projected annual growth % BR	=XIRR(E21:E22,E19:E20,0.1)*100
13	Risk Premium %	15		End-period Investment Value HR	=E24
14	Redemption Yld % pa 5-yr Gilts	2.66		Projected growth for period % HR	=(E13-B5)/B5*100
15	WORKINGS			Projected annual growth % HR	=XIRR(E23:E24,E19:E20,0.1)*100
16		0		**Share Intrinsic Value**	=E10*100/(100+B13)
17		0		**Value as % of Current Price**	=+E16/B5*100
18		0		WORKINGS	
19		0		Start Date	36526
20	End-Period Investment Value BR	=E9		End Date	38353
21	End-Period FTSE100 yield %	=+(B10/10.5*3)+2.4		Start Investment Value BR	=-B5
22	Last forecast year dividend per share	14.63		End Investment Value BR	=E9
23	No. of years not forecast	2		Start Investment Value HR	=-B5
24	Default actual dividend growth factor	=(1+(B12/100))*(1+(B9/100))		End Investment Value HR	=+E7*((1+(E8/100*0.75))^5)
25	Current Net Dividend	=-E3			
26	End-period dividend	=B22*B24^B23			
27	Actual dividend growth rate	=XIRR(B25:B26,E19:E20,0.1)*100			
28	Real dividend growth rate	=(100+B27)/(100+B9)*100-100			

Now that we have a valuation, how should we interpret this?

INTERPRETING THE FINAL RESULT

On the face of it, the valuation on 16 October 2009 showed International Power to be a strong buy. The intrinsic value was 179% of the market price. But you should never take default share valuations at face value; you should always carry out essential checks on the company before you decide to invest. These checks are described in chapter 13.

You are also advised to test how changes to the input data may affect the valuation subsequently. I will explain this scenario testing facility, which is a unique feature of the System, in more detail in the next chapter.

Let's test a potential worst-case scenario, in which all the relevant input variables change adversely. The two input values which will not change if you do decide to invest in International Power at this price on 16 October 2009 are the share price and the current dividend yield. Let's look at the impact on the valuation of changing the other input factors adversely:

- Increase average inflation to 3.39.

- Increase end-period inflation to 5.17.

- Reduce the end-period dividend to 14 (over-type the formula in B26).

- Increase the risk premium to 20%.

- Increase the redemption yield % p.a. on five-year gilts to 3.66%.

The combined effect of making all these adverse changes is to reduce the percentage valuation to 126.4% of market price. My minimum threshold for buying a share (it is lower for the FTSE100) is 115%. So, even with all these adverse changes, International Power still rated a buy on this date.

WHAT HAPPENED TO THE SHARE PRICE OF INTERNATIONAL POWER?

By Christmas Eve 2010 the share price had increased to 448.6p. This represents a rise of 69% on 16 October 2009, compared with a rise of just 15.8% in the FTSE100 price. Incidentally this strong rise, in addition to validating the valuation of 16 October 2009, shows two other points:

1. Most of the worst-case scenario changes had not occurred, e.g. end-period inflation remained around 3% and gilt yields remained low, far below the worst-case scenario of 3.66% p.a.

2. If a share is re-rated in line with a valuation from the System, the short-term capital growth can be very rapid and much higher than the projected annual growth figures shown in the System – these assume that the capital growth is spread out evenly over the five-year period.

SETTING UP A MASTER SHARE VALUATION SHEET

When you are satisfied that you have input the formulae correctly, you should delete all the input data values, except the dates in E19 and E20, and save this spreadsheet as the master share valuation tool under a file name of your choice.

Any subsequent valuations using this master spreadsheet should be saved under different file names to avoid the danger of new valuations being contaminated by data from previous valuations.

When you have constructed the master spreadsheet, you only need to enter the following data subsequently to obtain a share valuation:

- Cell B3: Date of valuation (factual)

- Cell B4: Share name (factual)

- Cell B5: Share price (factual)

- Cell B6: Share dividend yield (factual)

- Cell B7: Target dividend cover (projected)

- Cell B8: Actual end-period dividend cover (projected)

- Cell B9: Average inflation rate (factual)

- Cell B10: End-period inflation rate (factual)

- Cell B11: Real dividend growth rate (projected). [Supplemented, as required, by calculations in B27.]

- Cell B12: Default real dividend growth rate (projected)

- Cell B13: Risk premium (projected)

- Cell B14: Redemption yield % p.a. five-year gilts (factual)

10 | TESTING DIFFERENT VALUATION SCENARIOS

The logical way in which the intrinsic valuations are constructed enables you to test the impact on the valuation of changing the input factors, either individually or in combination. This is a very powerful feature.

ALTERING INPUTS IN THE FTSE100 VALUATION

Table 10.1 describes the impact of changing the input valuations in the FTSE100 valuation system.

Table 10.1 – Impact of changing FTSE100 valuation input values

Data input values	Impact of change on valuation
• FTSE100 price • FTSE100 net dividend yield %	No impact is applicable. Once you have made the investment, the price and current dividend yield are locked in. Of course the dividend can subsequently change – but that is covered by the real dividend growth rate.
• Average inflation rate • End-period inflation rate • Redemption yield % p.a. five-year gilts	In practice, it does not make sense to change one of these values without changing the others, as they are economically interlinked. Changing the end-period inflation rate is likely to change the average-period inflation rate (by around 50% of the change in the end-period rate, unless the change follows a crooked path). Also, if inflation is increased, gilt yields are likely to increase as investors seek inflation protection. In isolation, an increase in inflation will normally reduce the FTSE100 intrinsic value as the associated increase in the end-period dividend yield will reduce the end-period FTSE100 price for any given dividend. An increase in the five-year gilt yield will also, in isolation, reduce the FTSE100 intrinsic value, as it increases the discount rate and makes it comparatively more attractive to hold gilts than shares.
• Real dividend growth rate	This is the most potent input factor in the FTSE100 valuation. An increase in the real dividend growth rate will increase the FTSE100 intrinsic valuation and vice-versa.
• Risk premium %	An increase in the risk premium reduces the intrinsic valuation, and vice-versa.

IMPACT OF SAMPLE CHANGES ON THE INTRINSIC CORE FTSE100 VALUATION OF 3 MARCH 2009

You can verify these impacts for yourself by making the changes in the spreadsheet which you created earlier for this valuation (see chapter 7). Table 10.2 shows the impact of changing the input values for the 3 March 2009 valuation.

Table 10.2 – Impact of changing input values for the FTSE100 valuation of 3 March 2009

Data input values	Change in input value	Percentage change in intrinsic value
Average inflation rate	+ 0.5% nominal to 2%	In combination these changes reduce the intrinsic valuation by 9.5% from 5013.3 to 4538.3
End-period inflation rate	+ 1.0% nominal to 4.25%	
Redemption yield % p.a. 5-year gilts	+ 1.0% nominal to 3.41%	
Real dividend growth rate	+ 1% nominal to -5%	This change increases the valuation by 5.7% from 5013.3 to 5298.4

ALTERING INPUTS IN THE VALUATION OF INDIVIDUAL SHARES

The same scenario impacts occur when valuing individual shares as for the FTSE100 but there are additional input values, the variance of which will impact the current intrinsic value of the share:

- **Target dividend cover**. I use a fairly conservative target cover of 2.25. Some analysts believe that anything over 2 is acceptable. The higher the target, the lower the intrinsic valuation.

- **Actual end-period dividend cover**. A higher end-period dividend cover will reduce the end-period dividend yield and therefore, for any given dividend, will increase the end-period share price and intrinsic valuation.

- **End-period dividend**. An increase in the end-period dividend increases the intrinsic value of the share, in the same way as it does for the intrinsic value of the FTSE100. However, the range of potential dividend growth rates, from positive to negative, is far greater for individual shares than it is for the FTSE100.

- **Risk premium percentage**. An increase in the risk premium will decrease the intrinsic value of the share. Unlike the FTSE100, there is no long-term default risk premium for an individual share.

IDENTIFYING ONE-WAY BETS

The powerful scenario-testing facility can help you identify one-way bets. These situations do not occur often but, when they do, bold investors can make big money through the use of derivatives (e.g. covered warrants), whichever way the market is heading.

The more extreme the valuation, above or below 100%, the more likelihood there is of a one-way bet opportunity. The FTSE100 market peak of 6930 on 30 December 1999 presented one such opportunity (for short sellers or the buyers of put options). As identified earlier, the share valuation system calculated that the intrinsic value of the FTSE100 at this time was 4017 (58% of its price).

Let's run a scenario test on this valution, changing the variable input values in such a way as to deliberately reduce the overpricing.

BEST-CASE SCENARIO FOR THE FTSE 100 VALUATION ON 30 DECEMBER 1999

- **Inflation**. Assume that inflation falls sharply to 2% by the end of the five-year period. This is a reduction of 2.32 on the current market expectation and implies a reduction of half of this for the average inflation; this is 3.75 less 50% of 2.32 = 2.59.

- **Real dividend growth rate**. Assume that growth is going to be very strong over the period – double the long-term average, i.e. 4% p.a.

- **Five-year gilt yield % p.a**. Assume that the five-year gilt yield falls sharply to 2.5% because of the assumed fall in inflation.

The scenario changes are summarised in Table 10.3.

Table 10.3 – Best-case input value changes for FTSE100 valuation of 30 December 1999

Input value	Value on 30 December 1999	Best-case scenario value
Average inflation	3.75	2.59
End-period inflation	4.32	2.0
Real dividend growth rate	2.0	4.0
Five-year gilt yield % p.a.	6.09	2.5

If you make these best-case amendments to the FTSE100 valuation for 30 December 1999, the FTSE100 still remains heavily overpriced. The intrinsic value is still only 86% of the market price. The valuation spreadsheet is shown in Figure 10.1.

This is a very strong sign of an opportunity for a one-way bet. As we have seen, the market subsequently plunged, making great profits for short-sellers of the FTSE100 and for holders of FTSE100 put options.

Figure 10.1 – Best-case scenario valuation for FTSE100 on 30 December 1999

◇	A	B	C	D	E
1	**FTSE100 VALUATION**				
2	INPUT DATA			RESULTS	
3	Date	30-Dec-99		Current Net Dividend	141.4
4				Actual Dividend Growth % p.a.	6.7
5	FTSE100 Price	6930.2		End-period Dividend	195.5
6				End-period Dividend Yield	3.0
7	FTSE100 Dividend Yield %	2.04		End-period FTSE100 Price	6578.1
8				Average Dividend Yield	2.5
9	Average Inflation Rate	2.59		End-period Investment Value BR	7444.6
10				Discounted Investment Value BR	6580.0
11	End-Period Inflation Rate	2		Projected growth for period % BR	7.4
12				Projected annual growth % BR	1.4
13	Real Dividend Growth Rate	4.0		End-period Investment Value HR	7219.9
14				Projected growth for period % HR	4.2
15	Risk Premium%	10		Projected annual growth % HR	0.8
16				**FTSE100 Intrinsic Value**	**5981.8**
17	Redemption Yld % pa 5-yr Gilts	2.5		**Value as % of Current Price**	**86.3**
18	WORKINGS			WORKINGS	
19	Inflation Growth Factor	1.0259		Start Date	01/01/00
20	Real Dividend Growth Factor	1.04		End Date	01/01/05
21		0		Start Investment Value BR	-6930.2
22		0		End Investment Value BR	7444.6
23		0		Start Investment Value HR	-6930.2
24		0		End Investment Value HR	7219.9
25	End-period Investment Value BR	7444.6		Real Dividend Start Period	-100.0
26				Real Dividend End Period	
27				Real Dividend Growth Rate % p.a.	#NUM!

VALUE-BUYING RATHER THAN RANDOM-BUYING SUBSTANTIALLY INCREASES YOUR CHANCES OF SUCCESS

As you have seen, changes to the input variables, e.g. changes to the economic environment, will change the valuations of the FTSE100 and of individual shares. You should not fall into the trap of thinking that this makes calculating share valuations a futile exercise; just remember that it is important to stress-test for the possible impact of such changes.

You are far more likely to achieve investment success if, at the time you invest, the valuation supports your investment decision, whether you are a bull or a bear. The valuation, if diligently undertaken, significantly stacks the odds in your favour.

PART IV

PUTTING THE SYSTEM INTO PRACTICE

Now that you have built the templates for valuing the FTSE100 and for valuing individual shares, you have very powerful tools to undertake effective and profitable value investing. In Part IV I explain how you can put theory into practice and transform your financial security.

11

MEDIUM-RISK, HIGH-RETURN STRATEGY

Over the 27 years from January 1984 to December 2010, the medium-risk strategy outlined here has delivered a real return of 6.3% p.a. (10.17% actual p.a.) using ShareMaestro's FTSE100 valuations and the associated buy and sell signals. This is a considerably higher return than you would have achieved from most commercially managed funds. Over the decade to December 2010, the return achieved from this strategy was over double that achieved by the median-placed commercially managed equity fund.

THE PRINCIPLE OF THE STRATEGY

The basic principle of the strategy is to buy into the FTSE100 when the price is good value and to switch into instant-access cash when the price becomes poor value. Because of the time invested in cash, this strategy is lower-risk than remaining fully invested in the FTSE100 at all times.

Investment in the FTSE100 is via a FTSE100 exchange-traded fund (ETF), which aims to replicate the performance of the FTSE100 as closely as possible. It is impractical and far too costly for you to try to replicate the performance of the FTSE by holding an individual stake in all 100 shares in the right proportions – the ETF will do this for you for much less hassle and cost.

One of the most popular FTSE100 ETF funds is that run by iShares (**www.uk.ishares.com**). The fund pays regular dividends which can be reinvested in the fund. You can trade this ETF via any of the online dealing services which I cover in chapter 20. Standard dealing commissions apply.

Unlike other collective investment vehicles such as unit trusts and open-ended investment companies (OEICS), ETFs:

- generally have low management fees (generally 0.4% p.a. or less)

- provide exactly the price at which you are trading when you buy and sell (unit trusts trade on a forward pricing basis so that the price is set at the next price calculation after you trade).

You should ensure that any FTSE100 ETF which you choose invests fully in the physical securities which comprise the FTSE100. You can check this from the factsheet issued by the ETF provider. Some ETFs invest in derivatives which attempt to track the performance of the FTSE100. The use of derivatives leaves you exposed to default either by the ETF provider or by the issuer of the derivatives and this is a risk it is best to avoid.

FTSE100 ETF STRATEGY

There are three basic steps to this strategy:

1. Buy a FTSE100 ETF when the valuation of the FTSE100 first reaches 105% or above.

2. Hold the ETF until the FTSE100 valuation first falls to 95% or below.

3. At this point you switch your investment to instant-access cash.

You then repeat the cycle.

When you have accumulated dividends from the FTSE100 ETF of at least £1000 you should reinvest them in the ETF unless you think that a sell trigger will soon occur.

You may also want to consider exiting the FTSE100 ETF if a market freefall signal occurs, as described in chapter 17. You would then re-enter the FTSE100 via an ETF purchase according to the rules detailed in that chapter. There have only been two such freefall signals since 1984. On the first occasion you would have been already invested in cash because the valuation of the FTSE100 had already fallen to 95%. On the second occasion (21 January 2008) you would have avoided 593 points of the FTSE100 price fall by exiting into cash when the freefall signal occurred.

The buy and sell signals of this strategy do not occur very often and so you do not incur high dealing costs.

MAKE A NEW VALUATION WEEKLY AND CHECK THE FTSE100 PRICE DAILY

You should perform a FTSE100 valuation weekly, as described in chapter 7.

You should also calculate what prices the FTSE100 would have to reach over the next week to trigger the 105% and 95% entrance and exit signals (as applicable). To do this:

- Let's say that you have a valuation of 114.6% when the FTSE100 price is 5275.4. So the price would have to rise to 114.6/95 x 5275.4, or 6363, to reach the 95% sell trigger.

- Let's say that you have a valuation of 90.6% when the FTSE100 price is 5100.3. So the price would have to fall to 90.6/105 x 5100.3, or 4400, to reach the 105% buy trigger.

You should check the FTSE100 price every trading day (I suggest at some time between 2pm and 4pm UK time) to see if a buy or sell trigger point has been reached. If so, act on it.

DETAILED TRACK RECORD OF THE STRATEGY

The detailed track record of the strategy, showing every buy and sell point using the FTSE100 valuation signals, is included in this chapter. The valuations use the default values of 10% for risk premium and 2% p.a. for real dividend growth. You may be able to achieve even higher performance by using tailored inputs for real dividend growth at times of economic depression, as discussed in Part III.

The following points are relevant:

- As ETFs were not available in 1984 it is assumed that, excluding the built-in ETF charges, the price of the ETF rises and falls in line with the FTSE100 price.

- It is assumed that cash earns interest at the UK base rate less 0.5%, and suffers the basic rate of tax. This tax would not be payable if the ETF is held within a Self-Invested Personal Pension (SIPP).

- Buy/sell spreads, which are generally less than 0.03%, and dealing commission have been included in the overall estimated average charges of 0.30% p.a. This average takes into account the time invested in cash, when no ETF costs were incurred.

- Capital Gains Tax has been excluded from the quoted returns. The incidence of this tax depends on individual circumstances. It would not be payable if this fund were managed in a SIPP or ISA.

- B and S in Table 11.1 indicate respectively the buy and sell points for the FTSE100 ETF. H indicates *hold* when the fund is valued at the end of 2010 but no purchase or sale takes place.

- Every sell point realised a profit on the previous buy point.

- At every investment-switching date, the market value of the fund had increased compared with the previous investment-switching date.

There have been some paper losses during investment in the FTSE100 but no realised losses. For this reason the strategy is medium-risk in the medium term (five to ten years) but lower-risk in the long term (over ten years).

Table 11.1 – Track record of FTSE100 ETF strategy (medium-risk). Fund starts in cash in 1984 as the FTSE100 valuation was below 105%. Starting capital is 1000.

Investment date	Buy (B), sell (S) or hold (H)	FTSE100 valuation (%)	FTSE100 price	Investment exit date	Increase in capital (£)	Reinvested dividends (£)	Interest on cash (£)	Capital at investment exit date (£)
01/01/1984		103	1000	26/06/1985			110	1110
26/06/1985	B	105	1237	21/11/1985	185	17		1312
21/11/1985	S	94	1443	28/10/1987			185	1497
28/10/1987	B	106	1658	11/07/1989	534	121		2152
11/07/1989	S	94	2251	09/04/1990			144	2296
09/04/1990	B	105	2228	24/12/1993	1220	479		3995
24/12/1993	S	95	3412	07/03/1995			182	4177
07/03/1995	B	105	2977	12/10/1995	768	100		5045
12/10/1995	S	95	3524	11/07/2002			1755	6800
11/07/2002	B	108	4230	23/01/2007	3211	1587		11,598
23/01/2007	S	94	6228	16/08/2007			256	11,854
16/08/2007	B	106	5859	05/10/2007	1491	58		13,403
05/10/2007	S	95	6596	19/11/2007			70	13,473
19/11/2007	B	106	6121					
31/12/2010	H	108	5899		-488	1734		14,719

RESULTS OF THE STRATEGY

Table 11.2 – Results

Fund market value at 01/01/84	1000
Fund market value at 31/12/10	14,719
Compound annual return	10.47%
Net annual return, less average 0.3% p.a. ETF costs including management fee	10.17%
Net annual real return, less compound inflation of 3.64% p.a. (110.17/103.64*100) - 100	6.3%

Note: The average ETF costs of 0.3% p.a. is an overall average, given the time invested in cash.

TRADING THE FTSE250 TO GET EVEN GREATER RETURNS

The index for the next 250 biggest shares by market capitalisation, after the 100 companies in the FTSE100, is called the FTSE250. As the FTSE250 has smaller companies than the FTSE100, the index tends, over the long term, to grow more rapidly than the FTSE100. Smaller companies have the capacity to expand more quickly than the bigger ones. In the period covered by Figure 11.1 (6/1/94 to 17/3/11) the FTSE100 increased by 70%, whereas the FTSE250 increased by 195%.

Figure 11.1 shows clearly how closely the upward and downward movements of the FTSE250 correspond with the upward and downward movements of the FTSE100. The percentage changes of the FTSE250 are generally larger, although the directional movement is normally similar. Please note that, on the graph, the starting point of the FTSE250 has been rebased to that of the FTSE100. As a result, whilst the percentage price changes of the FTSE250 on this rebased starting point are correct, all the FTSE250 prices shown have been rebased pro-rata to the rebasing of the starting price.

There is at least one ETF which covers the FTSE250, provided by iShares. It should therefore be possible to achieve even greater returns than the FTSE100 ETF strategy by switching between FTSE250 investment and cash according to the buy and sell signals of the System for the FTSE100, but using the market-freefall exit risk control system (see next chapter) with moving averages for the FTSE250.

Figure 11.1 – Comparative price movement of FTSE100 and FTSE250 from 1994 to 2011

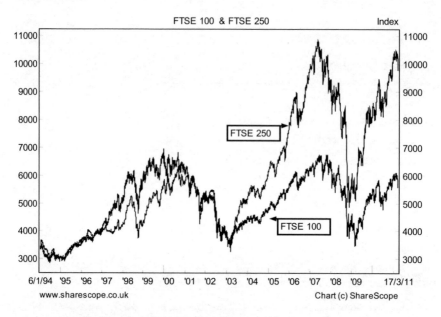

Source: ShareScope, **www.sharescope.co.uk**, © ShareScope

12

RUNNING YOUR OWN SHARE PORTFOLIO SUCCESSFULLY

We have seen in chapters 7 and 9 how you can produce intrinsic valuations for the FTSE100 and for individual shares. I explain in this chapter how you can use these valuations to manage successfully your own share portfolio.

The strategy described is for prudent investors who wish to limit their risk and seek to outperform the market over the medium to long term.

The steps required are as follows:

1. Time your entry to the market.

2. Draw up a shortlist of shares.

3. Select shares for investment.

4. Limit risk.

5. Set up email alerts for the shares in your portfolio.

6. Review progress and take appropriate action.

Let's look at these steps in turn.

1. TIME YOUR ENTRY TO THE MARKET

You should make a weekly valuation of the FTSE100. This takes a couple of minutes. You should consider investing in shares when the FTSE100 valuation is over 105% of market price. If you buy shares when the FTSE100 valuation is below this level, you run the risk that the prices of your shares will fall in a general market downturn.

2. DRAW UP A SHORTLIST OF SHARES

If the FTSE100 valuation is favourable, start to draw up a shortlist of potential shares for investment by getting valuations from the System. To allow a suitable safety margin, you should only consider shares with a valuation to market price of at least 115%. There are three ways you can select shares for adding to the shortlist:

1. Perform individual valuations for shares in which you become interested (for example, because of news items in the financial press) and add these to the shortlist, if the valuations exceed 115%.

2. Use the FT screener (**markets.ft.com/screener/customScreen.asp**) to produce lists of shares which meet the key quantitative criteria covered in the next chapter. Then perform individual valuations for shares which pass the screening process and add these to the shortlist, if the valuations exceeed 115%.

3. Use the ShareMaestro software (see chapter 20) to produce bulk valuations for all shares in the FTSE All-Share index. This is by far the quickest way to draw up a shortlist of shares. Add those shares with the highest percentage valuations to the shortlist, but ensure that you screen out anomalies. You should never take the raw valuations at face value without conducting further checks.

3. SELECT SHARES FOR INVESTMENT

Whittle down the shortlist of shares by reviewing the valuation for each share to exclude those with anomalies and negative factors, as described in the next chapter. Build an investment portfolio of at least ten shares, spread over several industrial sectors, allocating a roughly equal investment sum to each share. Shares are classified by the industrial sector to which they best fit (for example, Banks or Oil & Gas). Digital Look and other share data services provide the industrial sector for each share.

You will probably need to repeat this step on a number of occasions to find enough suitable candidates for investment.

4. LIMIT RISK

For each share purchased, place a trailing stop loss order at, say, 12% of the initial purchase price, for the maximum number of days available. If you set the stop loss too low, the sale of the share may be triggered too early because of a temporary drop in the price. If you set the stop loss too high, you may suffer unnecessarily high losses until the stop loss is triggered. I have found a stop loss of 12% to be suitable, although you could of course choose another figure if you wish.

With this trailing stop loss in place your stake in the share will automatically be sold if the price falls from the peak price achieved since your purchase by at least the amount of the trailing value specified. So, if you buy a share for 100p, the trailing value would be 12p. If the share price rises to 130p but then falls to 118p (130p – 12p) or below, it will be automatically sold.

This service minimises any loss on the share and also ensures that you lock in profit on the share rather than see it all evaporate with a sharp reversal in the share price. The service is available from brokers such as Barclays Stockbrokers (**www.stockbrokers.barclays.co.uk**), who will provide details on how this service works.

5. SET UP EMAIL ALERTS FOR THE SHARES IN YOUR PORTFOLIO

You should set up email alerts for each share in your portfolio to ensure that you get the latest news, announcements and other information affecting the companies. You can set up these alerts with the free Digital Look portfolio service. You may also want to set up alerts so that you are notified when each share reaches a specific price.

6. REVIEW PROGRESS AND TAKE APPROPRIATE ACTION

Review any alerts as soon as you get them and take any appropriate action. For example, if any company in the portfolio issues a profit warning, I would sell the share immediately, irrespective of the recent price history. Watch for warning signs on individual shares, as covered in the next chatpter.

Perform a valuation of the FTSE100 weekly to determine at what FTSE100 price the 95% sell trigger will occur. If the market price of the FTSE100 falls to this 95% level or lower in the coming week, consider selling your whole portfolio of shares, as a FTSE100 valuation of 95% or lower is a bearish signal.

In a down market the prices of most shares will fall. When you sell your shares, reinvest the cash in a high-interest instant access account. Consider repeating the share investment cycle when the conditions of Step 1 above are met.

- Revalue your individual shares at least every month and immediately for a particular share in the event of major news about the company (e.g. a takeover bid). For each share recalculate the price at which the 95% valuation sell trigger would occur. So, if the share price were 120p and the valuation produced by the System is 102% (122.4p), the 95% trigger would be reached if the price increased to 102/95 x 120p = 129p in that week.

- Consider selling any share whose price has reached the 95% sell trigger point. A modification to this strategy is to wait until the 145-day moving average of the price starts to decline, unless it is already in decline.

- Replace any share which you have sold from the portfolio using the above steps (except when you have sold all shares in the portfolio because the valuation of the FTSE100 has fallen to the 95% sell trigger).

- Renew any trailing stop loss orders before they expire. You can normally only set these stop losses for a limited number of trading days ahead.

- When cash dividends in the portfolio have reached £1000, reinvest these dividends in the best-performing share, unless you believe that you may soon sell the whole portfolio because of the FTSE100 valuation trend.

You do not have to follow this strategy robotically. For example, by using scenario testing you may decide to take early action on an individual share.

You may also take your own view about the impact of major news affecting a company. For example, if you believe that a takeover bid is going to be successful and the bid price is higher than the market price, you may decide to hold the share until the bid price is received.

ADVANTAGES OF THE SHARE PORTFOLIO MANAGEMENT STRATEGY

- You limit capital loss during market crashes.

- You re-enter the market only when it appears to be good value again.

- You earn interest on cash when you are out of the market.

- You invest in individual shares which you have assessed as being good value.

- The upside potential on an individual share is unlimited, providing both the market and the share do not become overvalued, but the downside is limited to the amount of the trailing stop loss (except in fast markets when it is not guaranteed that a sale can be achieved according to the parameter which you have set). So normally the downside of the portfolio would be limited to a 12% loss (excluding reinvested dividends) whereas the upside could be in excess of 50%.

- You minimise the risk on the overall portfolio by diversifying the investment across at least ten shares in different industrial sectors.

- You are exposed to less risk than if you were fully invested in shares at all times because you are invested in cash at times when there is most risk of the market falling.

- You should lock in much of the profit on a star performer in your portfolio, even if the share falls significantly from its peak.

13

OPTIMISING SHARE SELECTION

You will usually find quite a few companies which exceed the 115% valuation hurdle (if that is what you choose), using the default valuation process. You now need to sort the wheat from the chaff.

For a start, you should never take a percentage share valuation at face value. You may get a few valuations as high as 300% or 400% or more; you need to undertake some due diligence on each target share in order to eliminate anomalies and other adverse factors. The more research you do, the greater chance you have of avoiding costly mistakes.

In this section I explain the techniques which you should use to whittle down a longlist into a shortlist and eventually to a buy or sell list. These techniques are split into two groups:

1. qualitative evaluation techniques
2. quantitative evaluation techniques.

I will be explaining the techniques from the perspective of an investor who wants to buy shares. To obtain the perspective of a speculator who wants to short-sell or use derivatives to bet on the share price going down, reverse the logic where appropriate.

You should exercise your judgement in using these techniques. It is very rare that a company will tick all the right boxes. I have asterisked (*) those techniques which I believe to be the most critical.

With one exception, which I will highlight, all the information to which I refer is available free from Digital Look (**www.digitallook.com**) or the *FT* (**markets.ft.com/ft/markets/companyResearch.asp**). In particular, the *FT* site also has a very useful stock screener that you can use to select shares which meet your specific set of criteria from a large menu of options.

1. QUALITATIVE EVALUATION TECHNIQUES

A qualitative evaluation technique involves subjective judgement based on non-numerical information.

KNOW THY COMPANY*

Before you invest in a company's shares you should seek to know as much about it as possible. The more you know about the target company, the better. If you have personal experience, e.g. as a customer of the company, even better.

The best starting point is to read the latest Report and Accounts of the company, which will be available on the internet. The statements of the Chairperson and Chief Executive are always good sources of information, especially as they refer to the future prospects of the company. But you have to read between the lines, as it is rare, and an admission of failure by these individuals, for the reports to admit that future prospects are bleak.

You should also read the news items on the company, preferably for at least the last year. For example, Digital Look has a 'Top newspaper links' section. These links often give comments from brokers.

When you understand the company better, you can start forming your own views about the opportunities and competitive threats facing the company. These are factors which will influence the current value of the company.

QUALITY OF MANAGEMENT*

The single most important factor in the future success of a company is the quality of the company's management, especially the Chairperson, Chief Executive Officer and Finance Director. A sudden departure in any of these positions is always a danger signal, unless the executive has been genuinely headhunted for a better position elsewhere. Sudden departures from these positions generally indicate dissension at the top or a tacit admission that bad things have happened or are about to be revealed. None of these factors is good for the share price.

On the other hand, a well-respected CEO who has presided over increasing profits for several years is a good sign, especially if the latest report gives cogent reasons for the good performance to continue. Additionally, if a company has just recruited a new CEO with a proven track record, this could be a good sign.

DIVIDEND CUTS*

I would avoid any company which has recently cut its dividend or which has resorted to paying it in extra shares rather than in cash (scrip dividends). Dividends form a very significant part of the shareholder return. Maintaining or increasing dividends is part of corporate psyche. If a company has to cut or suspend its dividend because it cannot afford to pay it, this is generally a strong indicator that the company is in trouble.

As this is a qualitative analysis we are not concerned here with the amount of the cut – any kind of cut should be regarded as a warning sign.

TAKEOVERS

I would also be very wary of companies which have recently proposed or completed major takeovers. Many of these takeovers are vanity projects by the senior management and research shows that takeovers generally destroy shareholder value rather than add to it. The most obvious recent example in the UK was the takeover of ABN AMRO by the Royal Bank of Scotland (RBS).

There are instances where takeovers do make corporate sense. Ironically, the reverse takeover of NatWest by RBS is an example in this category.

PROFIT WARNINGS*

If a company has issued a profit warning in the last year this is a clear danger signal. Often all the bad news does not come out at once, as the embarrassed company leaders like to put a positive gloss on the negative reports. Frequently, additional profit warnings follow, leading to a further decline in the company share price. As a matter of principle, I would always sell any shares which I held in a company as soon as a profit warning is issued. This can be psychologically difficult because you are often sitting on a loss at this stage. However, you will normally save yourself from suffering even greater losses.

RIGHTS ISSUES

Rights issues are a way in which companies can raise finance. Extra shares are offered, generally at a large discount to the current market price, and then amalgamated with the existing shares when they have been sold. Rights issues can be a warning sign. They generally occur for three reasons:

1.   To finance takeovers (see above).

2.   To finance corporate expansion, instead of, or in addition to, increasing borrowing. You need to be convinced that the expansion will add to shareholder value when taking into account the dilution of share value which the extra shares will cause.

3.   To provide cash which the company urgently needs. This is another strong warning sign to avoid the company. A recent example is the notorious April 2008 rights issue by RBS. Shares were issued at a price of £2 compared with the prevailing market price of £3.50. Many analysts recommended that shareholders buy these new shares. One even said the decision whether to buy these new shares was a *no-brainer*. Within less than a year RBS was forced to accept government finance; the government took a majority stake in RBS and the share price collapsed to below 50p.

2. QUANTITATIVE EVALUATION TECHNIQUES

A quantitative evaluation technique is one which uses numerical data. In using this data you need to be careful. In assessing trends you need to be sure that you are comparing apples to apples. Sometimes, past earnings and dividends per share are quoted in dollars, euro or other currency, whereas future earnings and dividends are quoted in pounds sterling or pence.

DIVIDENDS*

Dividends are a key component of a company valuation and you need to check that the dividend components of the valuation are robust.

1. CHECK THAT THE CURRENT DIVIDEND AND DIVIDEND YIELD IS CORRECT

If the company has cut or suspended its dividend in the last year the quoted current dividend may be incorrect. For example, in 2010 when BP suspended its dividend because of the Gulf of Mexico oil spill disaster, it was still quoted as having a dividend yield because it paid a quarterly dividend and the dividends which had been paid in the previous quarters were included in the calculation of the dividend. This was misleading because in the coming year dividends for the comparable quarters were likely to be reduced or eliminated.

2. CHECK THE CURRENT DIVIDEND COVER

The dividend cover is how many times the dividend per share is covered by the earnings per share. If the dividend cover for the latest financial year is below 1.5, this is a danger signal – it shows that the dividend may be cut if earnings do not increase in the future. A low current dividend cover is generally associated with a high (and misleading) current dividend yield. Also, look at the forecast dividend cover for future years. Does it look reasonable or sustainable?

You should also look at the cash flow cover (see page 158). The cash flow per share should be well over double the dividend per share. If it is lower than this, avoid the company unless there is a very good reason why the cash flow for the latest financial year was exceptionally depressed.

3. INVESTIGATE A VERY HIGH DIVIDEND YIELD

If the current dividend yield is over twice that of the current FTSE100 dividend yield, alarm bells should be ringing. This normally indicates that the market expects the current dividend to be cut or eliminated; this will not be good for the share price.

4. CHECK THE PROJECTED DIVIDEND GROWTH

If the dividend is forecast to drop from the current year in subsequent years, that is a cause for concern. Ideally you should be looking for an unbroken upward trend in dividend growth, not just in the forecast but also for the past five years.

ShareScope provides the details of each broker's contribution to the consensus forecast plus the date each forecast was made. I would be sceptical of a consensus forecast which does not come from at least three brokers. I would also be worried if there were a large difference between the forecasts. More weight should be attached to the most recent forecasts, as they are more likely to take into account the most recent developments.

Finally, it is worth checking that the figure given as the consensus figure for each year of the forecast does actually equate to the consensus. Sometimes there are calculation errors and the consensus figure provided does not represent the average of the individual broker forecasts given.

EARNINGS*

CHECK THE CURRENT PRICE-EARNINGS RATIO (PE RATIO)

The price-earnings ratio is the price per share divided by the earnings per share. If the ratio exceeds 25 for the latest financial year, this can normally only be justified by projected earnings growth which is well above average. Conversely a PE ratio below 6 is likely to signal an expectation that the earnings will fall in the future. This is not normally good news for the share price.

CHECK THE PROJECTED EARNINGS GROWTH

You should conduct the same checks as described above for the projected dividend growth. Again, ideally you should be looking for an unbroken upward trend in earnings per share for the last five years and into the future.

CASH FLOW*

The quoted earnings of a company can be manipulated by various accounting techniques so some analysts prefer to concentrate on cash flow. Cash flow is broadly earnings adjusted for non-cash items such as depreciation and amortisation. A company which has negative cash flow, with no prospect of making this positive, is probably due for a sticky end. Like dividends, cash cannot be faked unless there is outright fraud.

If the most recent and the projected ratio of the price per share to the cash flow per share is above 15, this requires serious investigation. It would normally only be acceptable if the company had low long-term amortisation and depreciation costs.

SALES

Apart from effective cost control, sales are the main driver of profits. An important ratio is the *price to sales ratio*. This is price per share divided by sales per share (or market capitalisation divided by total sales). If this ratio is over 5, the share price probably does not offer good value, unless accelerated sales growth is expected. Some value investors screen for shares with a price-to-sales ratio of 1.5 or less.

BORROWING*

Heavy borrowing can threaten companies, as interest costs eat into earnings. It also increases risk, as costs will sooner or later rise if interest rates rise. A commonly used yardstick is the *net gearing ratio*. This is calculated from total borrowings less cash divided by total equity (capital and reserves). A net gearing ratio over 50% is a cause for concern, especially if interest cover is less than 2.

Interest cover is profit before interest and tax divided by the interest charge. High gearing is less of an issue with companies which have semi-captive customers, such as utility companies, and which can therefore raise prices more easily.

LIQUIDITY*

However profitable a company may be, it could go to the wall if it cannot meet its short-term obligations. The *current ratio* is aimed at assessing the liquidity health of a company. It measures the relationship of current assets to current liabilities. If the ratio is below 1 this could be a warning sign. If the ratio is above 2, this is generally considered healthy. Remember that current assets could be inflated by high volumes of unsold stock.

DIRECTOR DEALINGS

The directors of a company are in the best position to know whether it is worth investing in the company. Although they may present financial results in the best possible light for public consumption, actions speak louder than words. Obviously a pattern of recent share sales, with no purchases, is a worrying sign – and vice-versa. ShareScope gives very good detail on director dealings, including the deal type (rights issue, exercise of option, etc.). You can also get information on director dealings from Digital Look.

MOMENTUM

The momentum of the share price is a good, although not always reliable, indicator of the short-term future price movement of a share. Consequently, if you are considering buying a share, you should be ideally looking for an upward trend in the share price for the last six months. This is normally visible from the price graphs which you can get from any of the information sources which I have mentioned. These sources also provide data on the relative strength of the share to the market or to its sector.

14 TRANSFORMING YOUR PENSION PROSPECTS

INTRODUCTION

The principal catalyst for launching ShareMaestro as an investment tool for the private investor was the new pension legislation of 2006, which, amongst other changes, permitted employees to run their own pension plans and to enjoy the tax savings which were previously only available to the self-employed.

In view of:

- the complete inadequacy of the state pension

- the withdrawal of final salary pension schemes and

- the constant erosion of benefits from both public and private sector pension schemes,

it is becoming abundantly clear that private individuals must build additional pension funds if they wish to enjoy a comfortable pension income without having to work until they are too old to enjoy any retirement. If you are lucky enough to have an inflation-linked final salary pension entitlement, subject to specialist pensions advice, you should hang on to it. But you may need to supplement this pension to enjoy a comfortable retirement.

Taking responsibility for your own financial management is essential if you want to avoid the penury which could result from ignoring the pensions time bomb. Although pensions have become a hot political topic, you will not hear any politicians speak honestly about the dire pension prospects which many people face. Most of them probably do not fully understand the threat.

The meagre real pensions awaiting most workers are directly and mathematically driven by three key factors:

1. increasing life expectancy

2. poor pension fund returns

3. high fees levied by the fund management industry, who manage most pension funds.

By its very nature, saving for a pension is a long-term exercise. We are talking about pensions which some workers will not draw until 45 years' time, so it is important to assess the real market value of future pensions, rather than the inflated projections so beloved by the financial services industry. It is no good targeting a nominal retirement income of, say, £20,000 in 45 years' time if the ravages of inflation have reduced the purchasing power of that £20,000 to, say, £3000 in today's money.

Further, the lengthy periods involved mean that relatively small differences in annual returns can have a major impact on the ultimate size of your pension fund in the future. I have already shown (in chapter 2) how the 1.5% annual cost saving achievable from managing your own funds rather than suffering the high charges levied by commercial funds can practically double the market value of a lump-sum pension investment over 40 years.

In this chapter I compare the projected pension which the median performance of a commercial pension fund would deliver with the pension which you could expect by managing your own pension fund with the aid of the System. Because the comparative returns achieved by commercially managed funds are not available for periods in excess of ten years, I have used in the projections the returns achieved by the median performance equity commercial fund and the returns achieved by the FTSE100 ETF and covered warrants strategies for the decade ending 30 December 2010; i.e. the last ten years.

The returns for this decade achieved by these two strategies differ somewhat from the long-term returns since 1984, which are shown in chapter 6. For example, the FTSE100 ETF strategy real return for this decade was 5.3% p.a. compared with 6.3% p.a. for the period since 1984.

WHY MOST YOUNG WORKERS FACE PENSIONS PENURY

THE TYPICAL PENSION ARRANGEMENT FOR MOST WORKERS

Final salary pension arrangements, which provide a pension linked to the employee's final salary at their company, will be virtually extinct by the time that today's young workers retire. With the demise of final salary pension schemes, in the future pension saving will typically comprise of two stages:

1. Making annual investments until retirement age into pension funds managed by commercial fund managers. In an employer's pension scheme, employees will generally be given a choice of funds in which to invest. A self-employed person will normally invest in managed funds recommended by pension or financial advisers.

2. Using the accumulated pension funds at retirement to buy an annuity to provide an annual pension. There may be varying levels of inflation protection built into the annuity. The more inflation protection which is incorporated, the lower will be the starting level of annual pension. The annuity will normally be provided by an insurance company, opening the way for more high commercial costs, which will substantially reduce the amount of pension offered.

This pension arrangement is known as *money purchase* as the accumulated pension funds are used to buy an annuity which provides the pension.

PENSION PROSPECTS FROM COMMERCIAL PENSION MANAGEMENT

I have calculated the pension which young workers could expect through using commercial pension management for their money purchase pension.

STAGE 1 – ACCUMULATING A PENSION FUND

To calculate the real projected value of the accumulated pension fund (the first stage described above) I have made the following assumptions:

- *Current age*: 20

- *Age at retirement*: 65

- *Assumed annual salary*: £25,000, increasing annually in line with inflation

- *Assumed pension contribution*: £2,500, increasing in line with inflation

- *Annual real return on pension investment* (after commercial fund management fees and costs): 1.2%

The figure of 1.2% for the annual real return is the median equity fund return achieved in the decade ending December 2010. In practice, pension funds invest in a range of assets, including cash and bonds, which normally produce lower long-term returns than equities. It is possible that future decades may produce higher returns in equities but the prospects for the coming decade are very uncertain, in the wake of the deepest recession since World War II.

If higher equity returns materialise, there are likely to be higher returns also achieved by the System's FTSE100 strategies, for which I give comparative figures later in this chapter.

Using the above assumptions, the accumulated pension fund, after 45 years of pension contributions, will be worth **£149,797** in real terms.

STAGE 2 – CONVERTING THE ACCUMULATED PENSION FUND INTO A ANNUITY

To calculate the annuity which could be purchased with this fund (the second stage described above), I have made the following assumptions:

- *Age at retirement*: 65

- *Age of death*: 90[8]

- *Pension escalating by inflation*

- *Single-life annuity* (i.e. no pension payable to widow or widower)

- *No tax-free cash is taken* from the accumulated fund

In return for a fund of £100,000, the best single-life annuity currently available from an insurance company for a 65-year old male in normal health is £4301 p.a., escalating by inflation. Given the life expectancy of 18 years, this equates to a *negative* annual real return of 2.6% (you can check this via the Excel annuity formula given on page 65). Most insurance companies offer considerably lower annuities than this. For a life expectancy of 25 years, this negative return would deliver an annuity of £2831 for £100,000 or £4238 for £149,797.

£4,238 is just 16.9% of the average salary of £25,000.

If the real salary has increased by 50% during the worker's career to £37,500, the £2500 p.a. pension saving will buy a pension of just 11.3% of the final salary. As final salary schemes typically pay a pension of two-thirds (66.7%) of final salary for an employee who qualifies for the full pension, it is hardly surprising that final salary schemes have been closing at such a rapid rate.

ANALYSING OUR MONEY PURCHASE PENSION EXAMPLE

With the assumed commercial fund real return of 1.2% p.a., and the negative return of 2.6% on the annuity, a young worker would need an annual pension contribution of 39.5% of salary to enjoy a pension worth two-thirds of final salary, assuming that the final salary had not increased in real terms during their career. If the final salary had increased in real terms, the required contributions would be even higher.

In practice, the pension contributions to money purchase schemes are nowhere near 39.5% of salary. Employers currently pay an average of only 6.1% of salary into employees' pension schemes.[9] Under the new law for compulsory company pension contributions, to be introduced in 2012, the total mandatory pension contribution level will still be only 8% p.a. of salary (employer 3%, employee 4%, HMRC 1% via tax relief).

Again using the above assumptions, the 8% annual contribution level will deliver an annual pension at retirement of just £3,390 or just 13.5% of the real final salary of £25,000 p.a. The pension percentage of final salary would be even less if the salary had increased in real terms during the career.

One final depressing note: By definition, half the commercial pension funds deliver returns which are lower than the median return, some considerably lower. Similarly many insurance companies offer annuities which are considerably lower than the best-value annuity which I have used in this example.

Most employees in money purchase pension schemes will be severely disappointed, and probably surprised, at how little pension their accumulated fund will buy. Under final salary schemes, it is up to the employer to ensure that the pension scheme is adequately funded to meet the pensions due to employees. Under money purchase schemes, all the pension risk is transferred from the employer to the employee.

HOW TO ESCAPE PENSIONS PENURY

To escape pensions penury, you will need to take control, wholly or partially, over your own pension funds. It is one of the key purposes of this book to help you do this. I will now explain how you can transform your pension prospects.

TRANSFORM YOUR PENSION PROSPECTS BY MANAGING YOUR OWN FUNDS

By managing your own funds, you could dramatically increase your prospective pension. I will use the same assumptions as in the previous section of this chapter, except that the real return on pension savings will be the 5.3% achieved by the FTSE100 ETF strategy over the decade ending December 2010.

STAGE 1 – ACCUMULATING A PENSION FUND

Using the same principles as shown in Table 6.2 (medium-risk strategy) a real annual return of 5.3% produces an accumulated fund of £457,752 after 45 years' investments of £2500 per year in real terms. This fund is over 3.05 times the fund of £149,797 produced by the median commercial fund real return of 1.2% p.a., as shown in the previous section.

STAGE 2 – CONVERTING THE ACCUMULATED PENSION FUND INTO AN ANNUITY

Rather than purchase a commercial annuity, I suggest that you should self-manage this fund to provide an annual income. With a real annual return of 5.3%, a fund of £457,752 will produce an annual real income of £33,462 for 25 years before the fund runs out of money. This annual income is over 2.6 times greater than the £12,769 which the commercial annuity negative return of 2.6% p.a. would deliver for this fund value.

So overall the pension is nearly **eight times** greater than the annual pension of £4238 delivered by the traditional commercial managed fund/annuity route, as described in the previous section.

Alternatively, with the 5.3% real return, if the objective is to provide a pension of two-thirds of the average salary of £25,000 (£16,666), then the pension contribution could be reduced from 10% of salary to 5% of salary (16,666/33,462 x 10 = 5). This is a very low contribution rate and results from the high long-term return on investment which effective value-investing can achieve. However, you should review your contribution level if future real returns from the FTSE100 ETF strategy turn out to be significantly lower than those achieved over the last decade.

The projected returns from the high-risk, high-return strategy are stunning. Using the 19.3% annual real return achieved in the decade ending 30 December 2010, the annual pension payable for 25 years from the accumulated real market value of the fund after 45 years is an amazing £8,482,965. And this is from an annual real investment of just £2500. However, I would never recommend that you invest more than a small proportion (if any) of your pension fund in a high-risk strategy.

THE POTENTIAL ADVANTAGES OF SELF-INVESTED ANNUITIES

It is clear from the examples in this chapter that commercially available annuities offer very poor value compared with self-invested annuities which are effectively managed. *Under the stewardship of the best-value insurance company, your pension fund would be effectively losing 2.6% of its real value every year.*

The advantages of the commercial annuity are of course that it would continue to pay out every year if you lived to reach your century (and beyond). In addition, the annuity payable from the insurance company is guaranteed whereas the return achievable from a self-managed annuity is not guaranteed. However, the insurance company guarantee becomes worthless if the insurance company fails.

Nevertheless, you could plan for a much longer period than average mortality and still win out with a self-invested annuity. For example, if you increased the payout period to 36 years, i.e. to the age of 101, you could still draw annually over double the commercial annuity payment, assuming the real return of 5.3% p.a. were maintained.

A further advantage of a self-invested pension annuity (e.g. using a fund built up in a SIPP) is that, if you die, the remaining balance, less the prevailing rate of tax – currently 55% – passes on to your family. With a single-life annuity, when you die nothing is passed on to your family.

Until recently, in most circumstances, retirees were forced to buy a commercial annuity at the age of 75 with any balance remaining in your SIPP. That requirement has now been abolished, paving the way for self-invested annuities as a legitimate part of pensions and inheritance planning.

PENSION PRACTICALITIES

In this chapter I have been making the case for you to manage your own pension funds rather than relying on commercial fund managers and annuity providers. However, pension legislation or your company pension rules (if you are an employee) may prevent you from pursuing a full self-management strategy.

The legal, tax and corporate pension rules tend to change frequently. It is outside the scope of this book to cover every aspect of pension planning, which is a notoriously complex area. You should therefore take independent specialist advice before making any decisions on your pension. A few of the considerations are covered in the following paragraphs.

If you are a member of a company pension scheme, you are likely to have a limited choice of commercially managed investments as part of that scheme. However, most schemes allow you to make a number of investment fund switches a year without suffering a buy/sell spread. If, within the range of investments, there were a low-cost FTSE100 tracker fund and a cash fund, you could copy the FTSE100 ETF strategy by switching investment between these funds according to the System's buy-sell signals.

Furthermore, after gaining the maximum employer contribution to your company scheme, you could also open a SIPP with a low-cost provider (see chapter 20) providing the total contributions to the company scheme leave scope for further pension contributions to be made within your annual pensions contribution limit.

In the above examples of self-managed pensions, I have assumed that you use the tax shelter of a SIPP so that you do not have to pay Capital Gains Tax on realised gains. Within a SIPP, the historic returns of the FTSE100 ETF and covered warrants funds would be a bit higher than those quoted and used, since, within a SIPP, cash interest is not taxable whereas the track records of those strategies treat cash interest as taxed at the basic rate of tax.

The tax-saving benefits of SIPPs and ISAs are covered in chapter 19. Both can be used as vehicles for pension saving.

SAVING FOR A PENSION USING AN ISA

It is possible to build a tax-efficient pension fund via an ISA as well as via a SIPP but there are pluses and minuses to this approach:

- There is no tax relief provided on contributions to an ISA but withdrawals from an ISA are not taxed. For a SIPP, there is tax relief on contributions but withdrawals from a SIPP (except for 25% which is tax-free) are taxed at your marginal tax rate at the time of withdrawal.

- ISAs are more flexible than SIPPs:

  - You can withdraw funds from an ISA at any time but you cannot withdraw money from a SIPP until you are at least 55 (and this age is likely to rise).

  - There is no ceiling to the value of your ISAs.

  - You can make contributions to an ISA from unearned as well as from earned income.

- You can only invest up to £10,680 in an ISA in a tax year whereas you can invest up to £50,000 annually of your earned income into your total pension funds, subject to staying within the £1.5 million value cap.

SAVING FOR A PENSION USING A SIPP

Many employers operating money purchase schemes will allow you to transfer the value from your funds to a SIPP on retirement. You will then be able to operate a self-managed fund if you choose the right SIPP provider.

The projected values of self-managed SIPPs in this chapter do not take into account SIPP administration charges. Since these charges are normally capped, the percentage impact of the charges will vary significantly according to the size of your pension fund. As the current administration charge can be a maximum of £200 p.a. (Hargreaves Lansdown figures used as an example), and pension funds typically are measured in the £100,000s, the impact of the charges could well be less than 0.1% p.a. and would not materially affect the financial advantages of managing your own pension funds.

Historically the alternative to buying an annuity with your accumulated SIPP fund has been to exercise *income drawdown* for part or all of the fund. There are quite complex rules regarding the operation of income drawdown.

INCOME DRAWDOWN

If you only put part of your fund into an income drawdown plan, you may put more of your fund into income drawdown in subsequent years.

The maximum amount of income which you can draw from the income drawdown plan is broadly the amount of income which you could get from a single-life, level (non inflation-linked) annuity. So initially the income which you can get from the drawdown capital is likely to be no higher than you could get by using the accumulated fund to buy an annuity. However, the income cap is reviewed at least every three years and you can trigger an earlier review if you want. So, if the capital has increased in value at the next review point, the income cap will increase and it will continue to increase throughout your life providing that the capital value of the plan continues to increase.

Many pension advisers do not like income drawdown because it could expose you to more risk than if you were to take out an annuity. They argue that, if the capital value of your plan were to decrease, the income which you could draw from the plan would fall (possibly dramatically if your plan had been badly hit by a market crash) whereas an annuity will give you a guaranteed (and, with inflation protection, increasing) level of income for as long as you live. In short these advisors consider income drawdown to be very high risk. But, as I have stressed throughout this book, you have to distinguish between short-term and long-term risk.

On a short-term basis (the next five years) these advisers are right. If, over the next five years, you absolutely must have a guaranteed level of income from your income drawdown plan, and you have no other sources of income on which you could live, then it would probably be advisable for you to buy an annuity.

However, over the long term, all the evidence provided in this book suggests that you will be considerably better off managing your own funds via a self-invested annuity through use of one of the strategies in this book, such as the FTSE100 ETF strategy. And it is in the later years of your retirement that you are likely to need higher levels of income to pay for expenditure such as medical bills and care home or nursing fees.

Incidentally, to limit the short-term risk to your income, you should consider restricting your investment management strategies from the five years before retirement to a medium-risk strategy such as the FTSE100 ETF strategy rather than pursuing higher risk strategies such as the FTSE100 covered warrants strategy or managing a portfolio of individual shares.

FLEXIBLE DRAWDOWN

A new facility called *flexible drawdown* has been introduced from April 2011. Under this arrangement, you can make withdrawals from your pension plans, including the associated 25% tax-free cash, whenever you want. There are, however, key provisos:

- You cannot make withdrawals until you are 55.

- You must be already receiving at least £20,000 in pensions (e.g. from state pensions, annuities and company pensions) before you can make these withdrawals.

- No further contributions can be made to your pensions after you commence these withdrawals.

FOOTNOTES

[8] These figures are based upon a 65-year old man having a life expectancy of nearly more 18 years. A man's life expectancy has increased by 17 years in the last 85 years. It is therefore quite reasonable to expect another seven years to be added to life expectancy (taking it to 90) in the next 45 years, given the continuing advances in medical science. Women live slightly longer than men on average, so take account of this in your annuity calculations.

[9] *The Daily Telegraph* (27 October 2010).

15

EVALUATING FIXED-RATE, FIVE-YEAR CASH INVESTMENTS

You can use the System to assess whether, at a given point in time, a five-year fixed-rate pound sterling cash investment is likely to be more or less profitable than a five-year equity investment. At the time of writing this facility is especially relevant as cash interest rates are very low and private individuals are looking at alternative types of investment. This technique is best explained by way of an example.

BASIC RATE TAXPAYERS

Let's say that you have performed a valuation of the FTSE100 on 13 August 2010 as shown in Figure 15.1. Note that the real dividend growth rate has been assumed to be 0% because of the very depressed economic conditions.

Let's now assume that you can invest cash for five years at a fixed, after-tax, interest rate of 3.2% p.a. You are a basic-rate taxpayer. What is likely to prove the better five-year investment, the FTSE100 or cash?

Note that banks and building societies always quote interest rates on a gross pre-tax basis, so a quoted rate of 4% p.a. is currently equivalent to a post-tax interest rate of 3.2% to a basic rate taxpayer (4% less 20% tax) and just 2.4% to a standard higher-rate taxpayer (4% less 40% tax). FTSE100 dividend yields are quoted net of the basic rate of tax.

Figure 15.1 – Valuation of FTSE100 on 13 August 2010

◇	A	B	C	D	E
1	FTSE100 VALUATION				
2	INPUT DATA			RESULTS	
3	Date	13-Aug-10		Current Net Dividend	182.5
4				Actual Dividend Growth % p.a.	2.3
5	FTSE100 Price	5275.4		End-period Dividend	204.5
6				End-period Dividend Yield	3.1
7	FTSE100 Dividend Yield %	3.46		End-period FTSE100 Price	6627.6
8				Average Dividend Yield	3.3
9	Average Inflation Rate	2.3		End-period Investment Value BR	7785.5
10				Discounted Investment Value BR	7055.0
11	End-Period Inflation Rate	2.4		Projected growth for period % BR	47.6
12				Projected annual growth % BR	8.1
13	Real Dividend Growth Rate	0.0		End-period Investment Value HR	7481.9
14				Projected growth for period % HR	41.8
15	Risk Premium%	10		Projected annual growth % HR	7.2
16				FTSE100 Intrinsic Value	6413.6
17	Redemption Yld % pa 5-yr Gilts	1.99		Value as % of Current Price	121.6
18	WORKINGS			WORKINGS	
19	Inflation Growth Factor	1.023		Start Date	01/01/00
20	Real Dividend Growth Factor	1.00		End Date	01/01/05
21		0		Start Investment Value BR	-5275.4
22		0		End Investment Value BR	7785.5
23		0		Start Investment Value HR	-5275.4
24		0		End Investment Value HR	7481.9
25	End-period Investment Value BR	7785.5		Real Dividend Start Period	-182.5
26				Real Dividend End Period	
27				Real Dividend Growth Rate % p.a.	#NUM!

CONDUCTING THE ANALYSIS

There are three stages to the analysis:

1. Calculate your annual expected return from the FTSE100 investment.

2. Deduct annualised transaction costs from the expected annual return to get the net expected annual return.

3. Compare the net expected annual return from the FTSE100 investment with the annual return from the cash investment to assess whether cash or the FTSE100 is likely to prove the best five-year investment.

1. Calculate the expected annual return from the FTSE100 investment

From cell E12 (projected annual growth % BR) you can see that the projected unadjusted return from the FTSE100 investment for basic-rate taxpayers is 8.1% p.a. There are two possible adjustments which you can make to this return.

1. The first adjustment is to factor in a risk premium, which is not factored into the return in cell E12. For example, if you want to factor in the default 10% risk premium for the FTSE100, multiply the End-period investment value BR, shown in cell E9, by 100/(100+10). In this example: 7785.5 x 100/110 = 7077.7. Enter this value in cell E22 (End investment value BR) and you will see that that the projected annual growth rate in cell E12 reduces to 6%.

2. The second possible adjustment which you can make is to take account of Capital Gains Tax (CGT). CGT is not payable within a tax shelter such as an ISA or a SIPP, and even outside the tax shelter the payment of CGT depends on individual circumstances. Let's assume the worst case that the full 28% CGT is payable on the profits from this investment:

   - Excluding reinvested dividends, the costs of the investment for CGT purposes are the FTSE100 price in cell B5 of £5275.40 and the proceeds are the End-period FTSE100 price (cell E7) of £6627.60, making a taxable profit of £1352.20 (£6627.60 - £5275.40).

   - The end-period value of reinvested dividends is the End-period investment value less the End-period FTSE100 price or £7785.50 - £6627.60 = £1157.90. As dividends have been reinvested throughout the five-year investment period, an approximate calculation of the CGT profit on these dividends is to multiply the end-period value of reinvested dividends by half the percentage profit made on the investment excluding reinvested dividends. This percentage profit is £1352.20/£5275.40 x 100 = 25.6%. Half this percentage is 12.8%. So the approximate profit on the reinvested dividends is £1157.90 x 12.8% = £148.20.

   - So the total taxable profit is £1352.20 + £148.20 = £1500.40. The CGT payable is £1500.40 x 28% = £420.

   - So, excluding any risk premium, the End-period investment value reduces through CGT to £7785.50 - £420 = £7365.50. Enter this value in cell E22 (End investment value BR) and you will see that that the projected annual growth rate in cell E12 becomes 6.9%.

3. If you want to factor in a risk premium as well as CGT, use the reduced End investment value BR (7077.7) – which was calculated above as the End-period investment value – for the calculations in this section.

   - First calculate the taxable profit excluding the taxable profit on reinvested dividends: assuming a risk premium of 10% reduce the projected end-period FTSE100 price accordingly (100/110 x 6627.6) = 6025.1. Deducting the starting FTSE100 price of 5275.4 makes a taxable profit of 749.7, excluding the profit on reinvested dividends.

- As a result of applying the risk premium, the value of reinvested dividends is reduced to 7077.7 less 6025.1 = 1052.6. The percentage increase in value of the investment excluding reinvested dividends is: 749.7/5275.4 x 100 = 14.2%. Applying half this percentage increase to the value of the reinvested dividends gives a taxable profit on the value of the reinvested dividends of 1052.6 x 7.1% = 74.7.

- So the total taxable profit is projected to be: 749.7 + 74.7 = 824.4. At 28% the CGT on this would be 230.8.

- Deduct the CGT payable (230.8) from the reduced Investment Value of 7077.1 to get the final projected Investment Value – 6846.30. Enter this value into cell E22 and you will see that the projected annual growth reduces to 5.3%.

2. Deduct annualised transaction costs

There are no costs to be deducted from the cash investment.

For the purposes of the example, I will assume that the investment lump sum is £30,000. You should make appropriate adjustments for different amounts. If you invest in a popular FTSE100 ETF such as iShares, you are likely to bear the costs as shown in Table 15.1.

Table 15.1 – Total expenses of five-year FTSE100 ETF investment

Item	Cost, as a percentage of £30,000 investment sum
Buy/sell spread	0.03%
Dealing commission	[2 x £12.95 = £25.90], [£25.90/£30,000 x 100 = 0.09] Thefore: 0.09%
ETF expenses	[0.4% p.a. for five years] 1.99%
Total expenses	**2.11%**

In addition, you should include any extra account management costs which you may incur through making the FTSE100 investment.

Dividing the above total transaction costs of 2.11% by 5, you get annual transaction costs of approximately 0.4%.

3. Compare the expected annual FTSE100 investment return with the annual cash return

- Without any adjustment for risk premium or CGT the core expected net annual return from the FTSE100 investment at 7.7% (8.1% less 0.4%) is over double that of the annual cash return of 3.2%.

- With a risk premium of 10%, the expected net annual FTSE return reduces to 5.6% (6% - 0.4%) but is still considerably more than the cash return.

- Taking into account CGT but not a risk premium the expected annual net FTSE return is 6.5% (6.9% - 0.4%).

- Taking into account CGT and the risk premium the expected annual net FTSE100 return is 4.9% (5.3 - 0.4). This is over 50% more than the annual cash return.

Whilst you are locked into a five-year investment with cash, you can take profits early with the FTSE100 investment if the FTSE100 shows strong growth in the early part of the five-year investment period.

HIGHER RATE TAXPAYERS

This section considers only the first tier of higher-rate tax (currently 40%).

1. Work out the cash return post higher-rate tax. A post-tax return of 3.2% for basic rate taxpayers would reduce to 2.4% for higher-rate taxpayers.

2. Conduct the same calculations as described for basic-rate taxpayers but use the End Investment Value HR (cell E24) instead of the End Investment Value BR (cell E22). Enter the revised Investment Values HR into cell E24 to see the revised Projected Annual Growth % HR in cell E15.

16

EVALUATING STRUCTURED PRODUCT INVESTMENTS

Structured products, which are marketed by several banks and building societies, take a variety of forms. Often they promise a cash return linked to the performance of the FTSE100, measured against a strike price taken on the day the investment begins. Frequently the return depends on the price of the FTSE100 in five years' time. As the System projects the price of the FTSE100 in five years' time, it is ideally suited, in combination with stress-testing, to assess whether these FTSE100-linked products merit investment.

Two points are worth emphasising:

1. The product structures depend on derivatives issued by financial institutions. The products therefore involve a credit risk should the issuing institutions fail.

2. The products should be viewed more as a way of receiving enhanced interest on cash rather than as an equity investment. For example, you do not receive any dividends from a structured product investment.

Here is a typical example.

EXAMPLE OF STRESS-TESTING A STRUCTURED PRODUCT

On 3 March 2009 I was offered the following structured product by NatWest:

> The investment would start on 29 April 2009, when the strike price of the FTSE100 would be set. The latest maturity date would be 29 April 2014.
>
> If, at annual intervals, the FTSE100 price were above the strike price, the investment would mature and I would receive a 9% annual return (simple interest) on my investment plus my initial investment. So, if on 29 April 2010 the FTSE100 price were above the strike price, the investment would mature and I would receive 109% of my initial investment. If the FTSE100 price were still below

the strike price but had settled above the strike price by 29 April 2011, I would receive 118% of my initial investment – and so on.

Now the potential downside:

> If the investment had not matured in the previous four years and on 29 April 2014 the FTSE100 price were lower than the strike price, and if at any time during the five-year investment the FTSE100 had fallen more than 50% below the strike price, I would receive back my original investment, reduced by the percentage fall in the FTSE100 between that strike price and the price on 29 April 2014.

> But, if at any time during the five-year investment the FTSE100 had not fallen more than 50% below the strike price, I would receive back my original investment without any additional interest.

An added benefit was that the return was treated as a capital gain and was likely to attract a lower tax charge than if it had been treated as income attracting higher-rate tax.

To simplify my assessment of this investment proposal, I needed to assess the risk of the FTSE100 price being lower on 29 April 2014 than the 29 April 2009 strike price. If the risk of this situation developing was sizeable then I could lose money by investing in the structured product.

I therefore constructed a worst-case scenario on the valuation of the FTSE100 on 3 March 2009, which we reviewed in chapter 7. This is shown in Table 16.1.

Table 16.1 – Worst-case scenario changes for FTSE100 valuation on 3 March 2009

Input value	Value on 3 March 2009	Worst-case scenario value
Average Inflation	1.50	2.875
End-period inflation	3.25	6.0
Real dividend growth rate	-6.0	-6.0
Five-year gilt yield % p.a.	2.41	5.41

This worst-case scenario stress-tested a sharp increase in inflation and gilt yields. I did not change the real dividend growth rate as this was already assuming a far worse five-year negative growth rate than had ever occurred during the history of the FTSE100. The results of the stress-test are shown in Figure 16.1.

Figure 16.1 – Results of worst-case scenario valuation for FTSE100 on 3 March 2009

◇	A	B	C	D	E
1	**FTSE100 VALUATION**				
2	**INPUT DATA**			**RESULTS**	
3	Date	03-Mar-09		Current Net Dividend	209.0
4				Actual Dividend Growth % p.a.	-3.3
5	FTSE100 Price	3512.1		End-period Dividend	176.3
6				End-period Dividend Yield	4.1
7	FTSE100 Dividend Yield %	5.95		**End-period FTSE100 Price**	**4284.9**
8				Average Dividend Yield	5.0
9	Average Inflation Rate	2.875		End-period Investment Value BR	5477.1
10				Discounted Investment Value BR	4208.6
11	End-Period Inflation Rate	6		Projected growth for period % BR	55.9
12				Projected annual growth % BR	9.3
13	Real Dividend Growth Rate	-6.0		End-period Investment Value HR	5156.8
14				Projected growth for period % HR	46.8
15	Risk Premium%	10		Projected annual growth % HR	8.0
16				**FTSE100 Intrinsic Value**	**3826.0**
17	Redemption Yld % pa 5-yr Gilts	5.41		**Value as % of Current Price**	**108.9**
18	**WORKINGS**			**WORKINGS**	
19	Inflation Growth Factor	1.02875		Start Date	01/01/00
20	Real Dividend Growth Factor	0.94		End Date	01/01/05
21		0		Start Investment Value BR	-3512.1
22		0		End Investment Value BR	5477.1
23		0		Start Investment Value HR	-3512.1
24		0		End Investment Value HR	5156.8
25	End-period Investment Value BR	5477.1		Real Dividend Start Period	-100.0
26				Real Dividend End Period	73.19
27				Real Dividend Growth Rate % p.a.	-6.0

It can be seen that, even in this worst case, the price of the FTSE100 *in five years' time (End-period FTSE100 price)*, was projected to be 4284.9, some 22% higher than the current price of 3512.1.

I therefore decided to make the investment. I waited until the last minute in case there was a surge in the FTSE100 price which took the strike price on 29 April 2009 above 4284.9. The investment matured just one year later, providing me with a 9% one-year return, which was considerably higher than that available from a bank or building society deposit. By 29 April 2010, the FTSE100 price had increased to 5657.

Obviously I would have made a considerably greater return if I had invested directly in the FTSE100 but, as I stressed earlier, structured products are primarily cash rather than equity investments.

You can conduct similar stress-tests to assess the viability of other structured products where the returns are linked to the performance of the FTSE100.

17

HIGH-RISK, STELLAR RETURN STRATEGY

This strategy is only suitable for medium to long-term investment (five years up) because of the potentially large short-term fluctuations in market value. Over the 27 years from January 1984 to December 2010, this high-risk strategy has delivered a stellar real return of 14.5% p.a. (actual 18.7% p.a.). This is a greater compound real return than that achieved by any commercially managed equity fund over the last decade.

If you had invested £1000 in January 1984 it would have grown to £101,737 by the end of 2010.

The strategy uses covered warrants to invest in the FTSE100.

COVERED WARRANTS

THE BASICS

FTSE100 covered warrants are high-risk investments. Without active management and appropriate risk controls you could lose all of your investment. It is also theoretically possible that your investment could become worthless if the issuer of the warrants defaults. So this strategy should only ever form a part of your wealth-building strategy. You should take appropriate professional advice before investing in covered warrants.

Covered warrants provide an option to buy (call) or sell (put) an asset by a fixed date at a fixed price (the strike price). When the market price is above (call) or below (put) the strike price, the warrant is referred to as being *in the money*. The warrant price consists of two elements when it is in the money:

- *Intrinsic value* – for a call covered warrant, the intrinsic value is the difference between the market value of the underlying asset and the strike price, if positive. If negative, there is no intrinsic value.

- *Time value* – the time value is the premium paid for future profit opportunity if the market price moves in the right direction.

If the warrant is *out of the money*, the warrant price consists solely of time value as there is no intrinsic profit within the warrant price.

OTHER FEATURES OF COVERED WARRANTS

The essential features of covered warrants are:

- You can never lose more than your purchase price by investing in covered warrants and so you do not have to pay any margin.

- The buy/sell spreads are low – generally below 1% for index covered warrants.

- You can trade covered warrants through the same brokers as you trade shares and the dealing commissions are generally the same.

- The price of a warrant will usually change by much more than the price movement of the underlying asset – this is known as *gearing*. The gearing ratio or multiple is the relationship between the percentage movement of the covered warrant price to the percentage price movement of the underlying instrument. Of course this opportunity can also become a threat if the underlying price moves in the wrong direction. Hence covered warrants are high-risk investments. You therefore need to invest when you have the best chance of making a profit. Systematic risk control is essential to prevent permanent destruction of value.

- Covered warrants are short-term instruments, since expiry dates are normally less than one year ahead. The time value which you purchase is like a ticking time bomb; this value will erode as time passes. Furthermore, this value erosion accelerates as the expiry date approaches. This strategy is long term because of the risk controls employed, the specifications of the warrants to be purchased and the use of the System's valuations to purchase warrants at times when the FTSE100 price is more likely to rise than fall.

- Covered warrants provide no dividend income.

- Profits and losses generated by the closing of covered warrant positions fall within the Capital Gains Tax regime. No CGT is payable if the covered warrants are held within a SIPP umbrella. You cannot hold covered warrants in an ISA.

FTSE100 COVERED WARRANTS STRATEGY

This strategy leverages the power of the System's FTSE100 valuations by using the gearing of covered warrants. Standard FTSE100 valuations are used, using the factual market data and the default values of 2% p.a. for the real dividend growth rate and 10% for the risk premium. The steps are as follows.

THE STEPS OF THE FTSE100 COVERED WARRANTS STRATEGY

1. PURCHASE A FTSE100 COVERED CALL WARRANT WHEN THE STANDARD FTSE100 VALUATION FIRST REACHES 105% AFTER BEING BELOW 105%.

Place a stop-loss order so that the warrant is automatically sold if the value of the warrant falls by 25% from the purchase price.

The warrant strike price should be from 20% to 30% lower than the market price (i.e. deep in-the money). If you have a choice, choose the strike price nearest to 20% lower than to 30% lower. The expiry date should be the nearest available three to six months forward. On this basis, time value should form a very small percentage of the warrant price and the gearing multiple should be around 4.

If no warrant is available with these parameters, wait until one becomes available, providing that the standard FTSE100 valuation is still at least 105%. Do not buy a warrant if the spread between the buy and sell price is more than 1.5%. If the spreads continue to be wider than 1.5%, you could consider using instead the financial spread-bet strategy, which is covered later in this chapter. This is also a high-risk strategy.

2 . HOLD THE WARRANT FOR TWO MONTHS UNLESS THE OVER-RIDING CRITICAL RISK CONTROLS ARE TRIGGERED (SEE BELOW).

Sell immediately after two months if the standard FTSE100 valuation has fallen below 105%. Otherwise sell as soon as the FTSE100 valuation falls below 105% or sell just before expiry if the valuation does not fall below 105%.

3. IF YOU HAVE SOLD THE WARRANT BECAUSE THE FTSE100 VALUATION WAS BELOW 105% AT OR AFTER THE TWO-MONTH STAGE, REPEAT STEPS 1, 2 AND 3 AS SOON AS THE VALUATION NEXT REACHES 105%.

If the valuation remains at 105% or more at expiry, immediately purchase a new warrant in accordance with steps 1, 2 and 3. This warrant will normally have a different strike price and expiry date from the previous warrant.

4. HOLD CASH IN AN INSTANT-ACCESS INTEREST-BEARING DEPOSIT ACCOUNT(S) WHEN YOU ARE NOT HOLDING COVERED WARRANTS.

5. ONE MODIFICATION TO THIS STRATEGY WHICH YOU MAY WISH TO EMPLOY IS TO ADJUST THE FTSE100 REAL DIVIDEND GROWTH RATE (AND THEREFORE THE PERCENTAGE VALUATION) AT TIMES OF SEVERE ECONOMIC RECESSION.

This would change the FTSE100 valuation percentages and, therefore, the timing of the entry and exit triggers.

You need to check daily whether the FTSE100 valuation buy and sell triggers have been reached and take appropriate action (i.e. buy or sell the warrant) if they have.

CRITICAL RISK CONTROLS

There are two critical over-riding risk controls which operate irrespective of the FTSE100 valuations. These risk controls are vital because sometimes panic can drive a cheap price to become even cheaper. Although, over time, the underlying price will revert to fair value, it may do so too late – i.e. after the expiry of the warrant.

Therefore, you should sell the warrant when one of the following occurs:

- The *warrant price falls by 25%* (see stop-loss order in step 1). After the sale, wait until the expiry date of the sold warrant before reverting to steps 1 and 2.

    or

- When *the market is in freefall*. The freefall criteria are very demanding and have only occurred twice in the history of the FTSE100. On the first occasion the fund was already out of the market. The criterion for determining whether the FTSE100 is in freefall occurs when the FTSE100 closing price falls more than 10% below the price at which the 145-day simple moving average of FTSE100 closing prices has crossed, on its way down, the 242-day simple moving average of FTSE100 closing prices. Free services such as Digital Look will calculate moving average graphs according to your criteria (see below). Note that freefall trigger may occur when you are already in cash. If this is the case, wait until the two conditions below are met before you purchase another warrant.

If you sell a warrant according to the above market freefall trigger, you should buy a new warrant (following steps 1 and 2 above) when *both* of the following conditions are met:

1. The 145-day simple moving average of FTSE100 closing prices has crossed, on its way up, the 242-day simple moving average of FTSE100 closing prices.

2. The FTSE100 valuation is 105% or higher.

MOVING AVERAGES

A simple moving average (MA) is the average of a series of numbers. It is calculated by dividing the total of the numbers by the number of the occurrences. For example, if you have the closing prices of the FTSE100 for the last 100 trading days, the simple 100-day moving average is:

```
simple 100-day moving average = total of all the
prices/100
```

Moving averages are normally shown as line graphs. A line with an upward slope indicates an increasing price trend. Two or moving average lines for different time periods are often shown to demonstrate share price momentum. So, if the MA line for a short period crosses and rises above the MA line for a long period, this is taken as an indicator of short-term relative positive momentum.

You can get moving averages for the FTSE100 according to your choice of parameters from Digital Look at (**www.digitallook.com/charting**) or from ShareScope.

Figure 17.1 shows the trigger for the market freefall exit signal and the subsequent market re-entry signal in 2008 and 2009. The jagged line is the FTSE100 price. The line which begins and ends the graph above the other line is the 145-day moving average and the other line is the 242-day moving average. The 145-day line crosses and falls below the 242-day line on 11 January 2008, when the FTSE100 price was 6202. The FTSE100 price then fell by a further 10% to reach 5581 on 21 January 2008. This is the freefall signal to exit/avoid the market and sell your covered warrant position, if you have one.

The graph also shows the signal for potential market re-entry. This signal occurred on 10 September 2009, when the 145-day moving average crossed above the 242-day moving average and the FTSE100 price was 4988. As, at this stage, the FTSE100 valuation was 105% or above, you would have bought a new covered warrant according to the parameters of the strategy. Otherwise you would wait to buy a new covered warrant when the FTSE100 valuation was at least 105%.

As standard you should check the moving average weekly. Check it daily if a freefall exit or re-entry signal is close to being triggered.

Figure 17.1 – FTSE100 freefall exit and re-entry signals, using moving averages

TRACK RECORD OF THE STRATEGY

Although equity covered warrants have only been available since 2002, option pricing models such as the Nobel Prize-winning Black-Scholes system produce prices which are very close to actual market prices. It is therefore possible to calculate historic warrant prices and establish the track record of this strategy.

By employing this strategy since the birth of the FTSE100 in 1984, there have been 32 profitable covered warrant trades and 11 unprofitable trades to the end of 2010.

The full track record of this strategy, showing every individual trade, is shown in Table 17.1. You can see how £1000 invested at the beginning of 1984 would have grown into £101,737 by the end of 2010.

The returns assume:

- Round trip commission of £26 on each warrant buy/sell pair (i.e. a purchase and sale commission of £13 each).

- Interest earned on cash at base rate less 0.5%, taxed at the basic rate of tax.

- 1% buy/sell spread on warrant prices, where prices have been derived from option pricing. In volatile markets spreads may be wider.

- No CGT payable (this will vary according to individual circumstances and would not be chargeable within a SIPP).

Table 17.1 – Track record of FTSE100 covered warrants strategy (high-risk), with warrant stop loss and market freefall stop loss.

Invest date	FTSE100 price	Call warrant buy price	Call warrant strike price	Call warrant expiry date	Exit date	Warrant exit price (bold = stop-loss)	Interest or gain / loss on warrant	Fund value at investment exit date (start = 1000)
01/01/1984	1000	Fund starts in cash as FTSE100 valuation below 105%					110	1110
26/06/1985	1237	0.291	1000	20/12/1985	27/08/1985	0.338	153	1263

27/08/1985	1311				23/09/1985		7	1270
23/09/1985	1292	0.312	1000	20/12/1985	21/11/1985	0.448	529	1800
21/11/1985	1443				28/10/1987		254	2054
28/10/1987	1658	0.412	1300	18/03/1988	29/12/1987	0.448	153	2207
29/12/1987	1730				05/02/1988		17	2224
05/02/1988	1738	0.382	1400	17/06/1998	11/04/1988	0.418	183	2407
11/04/1988	1811				14/04/1988		1	2409
14/04/1988	1787	0.432	1400	16/09/1988	14/06/1988	0.476	219	2628
14/06/1988	1866				16/06/1998		1	2629
16/06/1988	1862	0.392	1500	16/09/1988	26/08/1988	**0.294**	-683	1946
26/08/1988	1772				16/09/1988		8	1954
16/09/1988	1767	0.392	1400	16/12/1988	16/12/1988	0.373	-121	1833
16/12/1988	1774	0.392	1400	17/03/1989	17/02/1989	0.647	1166	2999
17/02/1989	2043				23/04/1990		281	3280
23/04/1990	2159	0.593	1700	21/09/1990	22/06/1990	0.736	765	4045
22/06/1990	2379				03/08/1990		51	4096
03/08/1990	2285	0.583	1800	21/12/1990	20/08/1990	**0.437**	-1050	3046
20/08/1990	2157				21/12/1990		115	3161
21/12/1990	2164	0.513	1700	15/03/1991	15/03/1991	0.794	1705	4866
15/03/1991	2494	0.563	2000	21/06/1991	06/06/1991	0.527	-337	4529
06/06/1991	2525				07/06/1991		1	4530
07/06/1991	2506	0.573	2000	20/09/1991	07/08/1991	0.617	322	4852
07/08/1991	2597				16/09/1991		40	4892
16/09/1991	2606	0.563	2100	20/12/1991	19/11/1991	**0.422**	-1249	3643
19/11/1991	2463				16/12/1991		23	3666
20/12/1991	2358	0.503	1900	20/03/1992	20/03/1992	0.556	364	4030
20/03/1992	2457	0.503	2000	19/06/1992	18/05/1992	0.716	1686	5717
20/05/1992	2704				08/06/1992		23	5740
08/06/1992	2646	0.603	2100	18/09/1992	18/09/1992	0.467	-1321	4420

18/09/1992	2567	0.613	2000	18/12/1992	30/11/1992	0.776	1149	5569
30/11/1992	2779				02/12/1992		1	5570
02/12/1992	2764	0.603	2200	19/03/1993	02/02/1993	0.647	380	5951
02/02/1993	2900				06/04/1993		50	6001
06/04/1993	2832	0.593	2300	17/09/1993	07/06/1993	0.577	-188	5813
07/06/1993	2845				08/06/1993		1	5813
08/06/1993	2844	0.583	2300	17/09/1993	09/08/1993	0.697	1111	6924
09/08/1993	2986				07/03/1995		473	7397
07/03/1995	2977	0.623	2400	16/06/1995	09/05/1995	0.866	2859	10,256
09/05/1995	3261				11/07/2002		3644	13,900
11/07/2002	4230	0.895	3400	20/12/2002	20/07/2002	**0.671**	-3501	10,399
22/07/2002	3896				20/12/2002		120	10,519
20/12/2002	3890	0.814	3100	21/03/2003	20/01/2003	**0.611**	-2656	7863
20/01/2003	3779				21/03/2003		35	7898
21/03/2003	3861	0.784	3100	20/06/2003	20/06/2003	1.06	2755	10,653
20/06/2003	4160	0.884	3300	19/09/2003	19/09/2003	0.957	848	11,501
19/09/2003	4257	0.894	3400	19/12/2003	19/12/2003	1.012	1492	12,994
19/12/2003	4424	0.955	3500	19/03/2004	19/02/2004	1.015	790	13,784
19/02/2004	4516				27/02/2004		8	13,792
27/02/2004	4492	0.935	3600	18/06/2004	27/04/2004	0.985	712	14,504
27/04/2004	4576				10/05/2004		14	14,518
10/05/2004	4395	0.945	3500	17/09/2004	17/09/2004	1.09	2202	16,720
17/09/2004	4591	0.935	3700	17/12/2004	17/11/2004	1.105	3014	19,734
17/11/2004	4796				19/11/2004		4	19,738
19/11/2004	4761	1.015	3800	18/03/2005	19/01/2005	1.045	557	20,295
19/01/2005	4818				31/03/2005		134	20,429
31/03/2005	4894	1.075	3900	16/09/2005	06/07/2005	1.353	5257	25,686
06/07/2005	5230				07/07/2005		2	25,689
07/07/2005	5158	1.146	4100	16/12/2005	26/09/2005	1.383	5287	30,975

26/09/2005	5453				06/10/2005		27	31,003
06/10/2005	5372	1.156	4300	17/03/2006	07/12/2005	1.274	3139	34,141
07/12/2005	5529				17/05/2006		482	34,623
17/05/2006	5676	1.236	4500	15/09/2006	26/07/2006	1.393	4372	38,995
26/07/2006	5877				01/09/2006		134	39,129
01/09/2006	5949	1.216	4800	15/12/2006	01/11/2006	1.363	4704	43,834
01/11/2006	6150				16/08/2007		1314	45,148
16/08/2007	5859	1.236	4700	21/12/2007	05/10/2007	1.93	25324	70,472
05/10/2007	6596				19/11/2007		365	70,837
19/11/2007	6121	1.316	4900	20/03/2008	18/01/2008	**0.987**	-17735	53,102
18/01/2008	5902				10/09/2009		1756	54,858
10/09/2009	4988	0.995	4000	18/12/2009	18/12/2009	1.196	11056	65,914
18/12/2009	5197	1.005	4200	19/03/2010	19/03/2010	1.44	28504	94,417
19/03/2010	5650	1.045	4600	18/06/2010	05/05/2010	**0.784**	-23630	70,787
05/05/2010	5350				30/07/2010		0	70,787
30/07/2010	5258	1.31	4000	17/12/2010	17/12/2010	1.87	30234	101,021
17/12/2010	5871	1.390	4500	17/03/2010	17/02/2011			
31/12/2010	**5899**	Market value at 31 Dec 2010				**1.40**	**715**	**101,737**

RESULTS OF THE STRATEGY

Table 17.2 – Results

Compound annual return from 1/84 to 12/10	18.66%
Compound annual inflation from 1/84 to 12/10	3.64%
Annual real return	14.49%

FINANCIAL SPREAD BET STRATEGY

Another high-risk strategy is to use financial spread bets (also known as spread trading) instead of covered warrants to gain accelerated growth. As with covered warrants, you should take appropriate professional advice before investing in spread bets.

WHAT ARE FINANCIAL SPREAD BETS?

Financial spread bets are available for a wide range of financial instruments (e.g. equities, currencies and bonds). A spread bet is an agreement between a client and a spread bet provider to exchange the difference between the opening and closing price of a bet at a future date. If a spread bet contract is held to maturity, the closing price will be the price of the underlying futures market. The way spread bets work is best shown by way of an example. A spread bet on the FTSE100 is used in this example.

SPREAD BET EXAMPLE

On 18 March 2011, the FTSE100 price is 5718. I think that the FTSE100 price is going to rise over the next few months. I get a spread bet quote for the September FTSE100 contract, expiring on 16 September 2011. The quote is 5628 - 5636. The higher price is the buy price and the lower price is the sell price. The difference between the two prices is the spread. The spread is the profit margin of the spread bet provider. I decide to buy at £5 per point at the price of 5636.

Fast forward to 14 September 2011. Let's say that FTSE100 cash price has risen to 5968. The current quote for the FTSE100 September contract is now 5952 - 5960. I decide to sell my previous bet at the price of 5952. So I realise a profit of £5 x (5952 - 5636) = £1580.

THE ADVANTAGES OF SPREAD BETS OVER COVERED WARRANTS

There are four main advantages of spread bets over covered warrants:

1. Profits on spread bets are free of any tax (Capital Gains Tax or Income Tax). Equally you cannot set off any losses on spread bets against any chargeable Capital Gains Tax from other investments. There is also no stamp duty payable.

2. There is no commission. This is covered by the spread.

3. You do not have to cover your total exposure with the spread bet provider. So you can earn interest on the balance of your exposure via an instant-access interest-bearing account. So, in the above example, your initial exposure was £5 x 5636 = £28,180. But you may only have been required to provide an initial deposit of £5 x 100, or £500, to cover this exposure. You would, however, be required to provide immediate additional deposit cover for any losses incurred on your position.

4. The buy/sell spreads can be tighter than for covered warrants.

THE DISADVANTAGES OF SPREAD BETS OVER COVERED WARRANTS

The extra leverage provided by spread bets is a double-edged sword. Whilst leverage will magnify your profits, it will also magnify your losses. It is up to you to monitor your position and to provide any additional deposits to cover your losses. If you fail to do so, your position will be closed out at your expense. It is therefore essential to have a disciplined exit strategy.

The pricing of the bets can be more volatile than those of the underlying futures market. As with other forms of betting, the prices are set by the betting firm and do not necessarily follow exactly the prices of the underlying instruments (futures).

EQUITY FUTURES AND HOW THEIR PRICES ARE DERIVED

An equity futures contract on a share/index is a contract to buy or sell the share/index at a specific future date at a price agreed at the time of the contract. The price of the equity future is derived from the price of the underlying share/index adjusted for two factors:

1. The interest benefit that the buyer of the contract will receive from postponing the purchase of the equity from contract date to the future exercise date (hence this benefit is added to the price of the cash equity to derive the futures price).

2. The loss which the buyer of the contract will suffer through not receiving any dividends payable between contract date and the future exercise date (hence this loss will be deducted from the price of the cash equity to derive the futures price).

THE MECHANICS OF OPERATING A FINANCIAL SPREAD BETTING ACCOUNT

This is a summary of the current procedures operated by Barclays Stockbrokers through City Index Limited. You should check the full details and requirements before operating a spread betting account with any spread betting firm.

1. You will need to open a financial spread betting account with a spread-betting firm, subject to their vetting and acceptance procedures.

2. When the account is opened you will be given online account access details. You can then acquaint yourself with the way that the market works.

3. You should understand the spreads operated by the firm. These may vary according to the time of trading, but, on a FTSE100 contract, the maximum spread (the difference between buy and sell price) will be in the region of 0.15%.

4. Stop losses are essential for an effective exit strategy. Stop losses aim to sell your position at a price specified by you if the bet price falls to that level. These are two basic types – *guaranteed* and *non-guaranteed*. At times of market panic, with a standard stop-loss, it may not be possible to execute the exit price which you have stipulated. A guaranteed stop-loss guarantees that the spread betting firm will honour your specified exit price. I would always opt for the guaranteed stop loss, as the premium for this option is small. On a FTSE100 contract it is currently triple your pounds per point bet. So, in the example above, you would pay £15 premium for a guaranteed stop loss – only 0.05% of the total exposure of £28,180.

5. You should understand the range of contract expiry dates available. These should be quoted on the dealing screen. Barclays/City Index currently offer the next two quarters of March, June, September and December, which have expiry dates on the third Friday of the month.

6. You should make arrangements to meet the deposit (margin) requirements of the spread-betting firm. For a FTSE100 contract, Barclays/City Index currently require an initial deposit of 100 times the pounds per point bet; thereafter any losses accumulating on your position must be fully covered by further deposits.

7. Spread bets often continue to trade when the cash markets are closed.

ADAPTING THE FTSE100 COVERED WARRANTS STRATEGY FOR FINANCIAL SPREAD BETTING

Please note that the bets to which I refer below are quarterly bets rather than rolling bets.

The following steps are required to implement via spread betting a similar strategy to the FTSE100 covered warrants strategy:

1. Place a *buy* bet on a FTSE100 spread bet contract when the standard FTSE100 valuation first reaches 105% after being below 105%. The contract expiry date should be at least three months from the purchase date, but as close to three months as possible.

2. Establish the amount which you have available for placing on the spread bet. Determine the amount of leverage or gearing which you wish to achieve. If you have no gearing, you will get no accelerated growth. If you have too much gearing, a small drop in price of the bet could wipe out most of your investment. A gearing of about 4.5 is in line with the covered warrants strategy.

3. Multiply your betting amount by your chosen gearing. So, if you have chosen gearing of 4.5 and the amount which you wish to bet is £20,000, the result would be £90,000. This is the maximum amount which you could lose without a guaranteed stop loss in place.

4. Divide your maximum exposure (in this case £90,000) by the current contract buy price to determine the amount of your stake for each point movement in the index. So, if the current buy price for your chosen FTSE100 contract were 5620, you would divide £90,000 by 5620. In this case the answer is £16 per point, with a bit of cash left over. Your total exposure would be £16 x 5620 = £89,920.

5. Determine at what price you should set a guaranteed stop loss order. Divide your chosen stop loss percentage fall trigger by your chosen level of gearing to determine the price to which the contract price would have to fall to trigger a sale. So, if you follow the 25% stop loss in the covered warrants strategy, you would divide 25 by 4.5 (5.555) to determine the percentage fall from the buy price at which to set the stop loss.

   So, if the buy price were 5620, you would set the stop loss price at 5.555% less than 5620, or 5308. If the guaranteed stop loss were triggered you would lose (5620 - 5308) x £16 = £4992. This equates to a loss of 24.96% on the £20,000, which is very slightly less than 25% of your bet of £20,000 (because your exposure was £89,920 rather than £90,000 since you cannot bet fractions of a pound per point). Don't forget also that the guaranteed stop loss fee of £16 per point x 3, or £48, will also add to your loss.

6. Provide the initial deposit (margin) required by the betting firm. For administrative convenience, you may wish to provide at least double the initial requirement to avoid the need to top up the margin immediately to cover losses which may be incurred.

7. Place your bet, including the guaranteed stop loss.

8. Hold your bet position for two months unless the stop loss is triggered or the covered warrants market freefall criteria, as described in the FTSE100 covered warrants strategy, are triggered. Sell immediately at the two-month stage if the standard FTSE100 valuation has fallen below 105%. Otherwise sell as soon thereafter as the FTSE100 valuation falls below 105%. Sell just before expiry if the valuation does not fall below 105% and immediately place a new spread bet in accordance with steps 1 to 8.

9. If you have sold the warrant because the FTSE100 valuation was below 105% at or after the two-month stage, repeat steps 1 to 8 as soon as the valuation next reaches 105%.

10. If your position has been sold because your stop loss has been triggered, wait until the expiry of the sold contract before assessing whether to place a new bet in accordance with steps 1 to 8.

11. If you have sold your position because the covered warrant market freefall criteria have been triggered, wait until the market re-entry criteria (following a market freefall exit), as described in the FTSE100 covered warrants strategy, have been met.

12. Hold cash in an instant-access interest-bearing deposit account(s) when you are not holding a spread bet position. Also, when you are holding a spread bet position, hold in this account any cash which is not needed for margin requirements.

13. One modification to this strategy which you may wish to employ is to adjust the FTSE100 real dividend growth rate (and therefore the percentage valuation) at times of severe economic recession. This will change the FTSE100 valuation percentages (see Chapter 7).

Due to historic spread bet pricing data not being available, I have not been able to construct a track record for this spread betting strategy. However, I would expect the results to be similar to those of the covered warrant strategy, subject to the availability of suitable contracts and the employment of similar gearing ratios.

One final point – as with covered warrants, you are exposed to the risk of default by the spread betting firm. You should therefore satisfy yourself on the financial soundness of the firm before engaging in any transactions.

A POSSIBLE MODIFICATION TO STOP LOSSES

This modification applies to both the covered warrants and the spread bet strategies.

The stock market opens at 8am. Between 8am and 9am prices can be volatile and spreads wide as market-makers react to overnight news from other markets. A stop loss can be prematurely triggered by an artificially low price during this period. A possible way of countering this risk, but only if you have the time and discipline, is to adjust your stop loss overnight to 30% *if the FTSE100 price is falling and approaching the 25% loss trigger* and then reinstate the 25% stop-loss as soon after 9am as possible. This should help prevent your position being prematurely sold during the volatile 8am to 9am period.

PART V

INVESTMENT ESSENTIALS

18 ESTABLISHING YOUR INVESTMENT OBJECTIVES

Before you start value investing you must determine what your investment objectives are.

DETERMINING AND MONITORING YOUR OVERALL INVESTMENT OBJECTIVES

OVERALL TARGET OBJECTIVE

As with any other objective in life, you are far more likely to achieve your investing objective if you define it clearly and establish a target timescale.

As I have previously emphasised, the financial dimension to any investment objective must be expressed in real terms. So any financial objectives must be revised each year in line with inflation (preferably your personal inflation rate). Sample objectives might be:

- I want to retire at age 60 and build up a fund from which I can draw a pension of £20,000 p.a.

- I want to invest to finance a deposit of £50,000 to buy a house in ten years' time.

- I want to build up a fund in 20 years' time from which I can draw £15,000 per year for the rest of my life.

The financial targets above are all expressed in real terms.

MONITORING PROGRESS TOWARDS YOUR INVESTMENT OBJECTIVE

It is essential that you regularly monitor the progress which your investments are making towards achieving your objective(s). I recommend that you maintain on a spreadsheet a balance sheet of all your assets and liabilities. The market value of your investments must be updated regularly as should any changes to the other components of the balance sheet.

The service providers which I detail in the next chapter all have online systems and portfolio tools which provide up-to-date valuations of your equity investments. You may need to adjust your tactics to achieve your objective (e.g. annual amount saved) in the light of the investment performance.

YOUR OTHER INVESTMENT OBJECTIVES

TIME HORIZON

Your overall objective(s) you may include both short-term and long-term financial goals. Remember that value investing is not normally suitable for investors with time horizons of less than five years. Share prices which are out of line with intrinsic values will, over time, revert to fair value but this can occasionally take more than three years.

RISK APPETITE

You need to determine your appetite for risk. Your objective should be, at minimum, to increase the real value of your investments. Measured against this, there is no such thing as a risk-free objective. However, it is possible to moderate the risk you are taking in your choices of how you will invest – what assets you invest in – and how long you invest for.

HOW TIMESCALE AFFECTS RISK

Timescale is important because over the long term (at least ten years), past experience suggests that there is likely to be far less risk to your capital from effective value investing in equities than from investing in cash deposits. Cash may give the illusion of growth, as the nominal value of the cash invested increases. However, the real value of a cash investment frequently declines.

Over the short term (less than five years) the balance of risk changes. UK equity markets can crash by 40% or more in two or three years, although the System should help you avoid the worst impact of these crashes. Crashes generally occur when the market is significantly over-priced.

Consequently, if you have a specific date objective to reach a long-term goal, it could make sense to reduce the exposure to equities in the last five years in favour of, say, fixed-rate cash deposits, so that you insulate your long-term fund against the impact of a short-term crash in the final years towards maturity of your fund.

CHOICE BETWEEN RISK AND REWARD FOR VALUE-INVESTING STRATEGIES

With the value investing time horizons of five years or more, there are different degrees of risk and reward. An obvious example is the difference between the FTSE100 ETF strategy and the FTSE100 covered warrants strategy. As far as reward is concerned, the covered warrants strategy has delivered a long-term real return of 14.49% p.a., whereas the ETF strategy has delivered a long-term real return of 6.30% p.a.

Both these returns far exceed the long-term real returns achieved by virtually all commercially managed funds. However, the difference in long-term capital accumulation is huge. Over the 27 years since 1984, the covered warrants strategy has accumulated a capital sum which is over seven times greater than that of the ETF fund.

But as regards short-term risk the ETF fund wins hands down. The market value of the fund has always increased on the implementation of any buy or sell signal, whereas in one six-month period the covered warrants fund realised a loss of 43%, even with stop-loss controls in place. The fact that all of this loss was recovered within 15 months would have been of little comfort to a risk-averse investor who had already thrown in the towel.

EFFORT

You also need to decide how much effort you are prepared to devote to securing your financial future.

To implement one of the FTSE100 strategies which I have mentioned should take no more than 80 minutes per week.

To manage a share portfolio of ten shares effectively will take about 30 minutes per week for maintenance plus from 30 minutes to two hours for every share which you decide to place in the portfolio. To reduce the effort of successful share investment, you may wish to subscribe to ShareMaestro and ShareScope (see pages 231 to 232).

SETTING YOUR INVESTMENT TARGETS

SET UP AN EMERGENCY FUND

Before financing any equity investment, you should decide how much money you need to reserve for an emergency fund. This is designed to ensure that you do not have to sell your equity investments at distressed prices in order to fund an emergency (such as losing your job). This decision must be personal because it depends partly on your risk appetite and partly on your security of employment. Personally I prefer an emergency fund equivalent to two years' total living expenses.

Only after reserving your emergency fund, which should be held in investments which carry low short-term risk (e.g. cash deposits with banks or building societies covered by the FSA compensation scheme) should you consider investment in equities.

DETERMINING HOW MUCH YOU NEED TO INVEST

You can use Tables 6.2 and 6.3 to determine approximately how much you may have to invest in equities, either as a lump sum or annually, to achieve your investment target, which should be expressed in real terms. A lump sum may come from a severance payment, inheritance or the proceeds of a maturing insurance policy, for example.

Firstly decide which level of risk suits you and refer to the appropriate time period in Tables 6.2 and 6.3. I would never advise devoting all your investment to the high-risk strategy.

For example, let's say you want a fund worth £100,000 in today's value in 20 years' time. Table 18.1 shows the projected real investment values for 20 years hence, assuming the same real returns as have been achieved over the last 27 years by the FTSE100 strategies. In this example we have assumed, as in chapter 6, an annual investment of £2500 as this is 10% of the average salary.

Table 18.1 – Real savings values after 20 years with medium-risk and high-risk FTSE100 strategies

Strategy risk	£2500 lump sum	£2500 annually
Medium: 6.3% p.a.	£8484	£100,970
High: 14.49% p.a.	£37,436	£276,041

This means the required amounts to be saved are as follows:

ANNUAL SAVINGS

- Medium-risk: 100,000/100,970 x £2500 = £2476

- High-risk: 100,000/276,041 x £2500 = £906

LUMP SUM SAVINGS:

- Medium-risk: 100,000/8484 x 2500 = £29,467

- High-risk: 100,000/37,436 x 2500 = £6678

You could also combine a mixture of lump-sum and regular saving.

FREEING UP MONEY FOR INVESTMENT

If you do not think that you can spare any of your current income for regular investment, you should investigate how you can reduce your expenses to free up funds. In 1992 I published a book called *The Personal Prosperity Plan*. This book explained how you could reduce your expenses (including taxes) by thousands of pounds per year. It then suggested how you could invest those savings effectively to build up a personal fortune. The book was ahead of its time but the principles still hold true. I could not find a publisher and so I published it myself. I am afraid that this venture had a negative effect on my own personal prosperity because the costs of advertising the book in the national press far outweighed the proceeds from sales.

Today you do not need to buy a book to find out how to free up money from your income to finance regular savings. Websites such as **www.moneysavingexpert.com** provide regular updates on how to save money. That website also sends out a weekly email containing the latest tips.

You can also free up money by using tax breaks, as I describe in the next chapter.

19

TAKING ADVANTAGE OF TAX BREAKS

Tax, principally Income Tax and Capital Gains Tax, can substantially erode the returns which you make from equity investment, but there are a number of ways in which you can mitigate or avoid tax. This chapter covers the main tax-saving opportunities for investors. These include:

- Self-Invested Personal Pensions (SIPPs)

- Individual Savings Accounts (ISAs)

- aditional voluntary contributions (AVCs)

- spread betting

- a range of other tax allowances and planning devices.

The nature of the topic means that only summarised information can be provided here. You should seek professional advice to determine the current figures and tax law, and the applicability of the tax-saving opportunities to your situation. Current tax information is available from Her Majesty's Revenue and Customs (**www.hmrc.gov.uk**).

Figures quoted are those applicable for the tax year commencing 6 April 2011.

SELF-INVESTED PERSONAL PENSIONS (SIPPS)

SIPPs are designed to allow you to build up a pension fund with tax-free growth; no Capital Gains Tax or Income Tax is payable within SIPP investments. Cash interest can therefore be paid gross within a SIPP. You cannot, however, claim back the 10% tax credit on dividends but higher-rate taxpayers are not liable for any higher-rate tax. You can hold a much wider range of investments in a SIPP than you can in an ISA. For example, you can hold covered warrants.

There are significant tax incentives on the money which you invest in a SIPP. For every £4000 which you contribute to a SIPP, a tax benefit of £1000 is added. Furthermore, if you are a higher-rate (40%) taxpayer, you can claim back a further £1000 through your tax return up to the amount of the higher-rate tax which you have paid. If you are a super-rate (50%) taxpayer, you can claim a further £500, on top of the higher-rate tax reclaim – again up to the level of the super-rate tax which you have paid. So a SIPP investment of £5000 can cost a higher-rate taxpayer only a net £3000 (£4000 less £1000) or a super-rate taxpayer only a net £2500 (£4000 less £1500).

But there are also limits to how much you can invest. Broadly, up to the age of 75, you can invest up to the amount you earn, with a maximum of £50,000 per year. This maximum includes personal, employee and employer contributions as well as benefits built up in final salary pensions. So, if you are a member of a company pension scheme, you need to check with your employer how much spare capacity is available.

If you do not use your £50,000 allowance fully in one tax year, you can carry the spare capacity forward up to three tax-years. Those without any earnings can invest up to £3600 in any tax year. You need to be careful if you are retired and have secured enhanced protection for your pension fund so that you do not have to pay any tax if the value of the fund exceeds the lifetime allowance (see below). Any further pension contribution will nullify this protection.

From April 2012, there will be a lifetime allowance limit of £1.5 million (currently £1.8 million) on the value of your pensions from all sources (including those in payment). If all your pension funds, including your SIPP, exceed the lifetime allowance when you draw benefits, you will probably incur a tax charge on the excess.

The main drawback with SIPP investments is that you cannot draw on them until you are 55 (and this age might be increased in future in line with the general trend of increasing the age at which pensions can be drawn). When you do start drawing benefits from your SIPP, you can draw 25% of the value drawn down tax-free. After this, the income which you draw from your fund is taxable at your applicable marginal tax rate when you receive the income.

As discussed in chapter 14, the rule that required you to convert any SIPP fund remaining at the age of 75 into an annuity has now been changed. There could be significant benefits to continuing to manage your SIPP funds, using the strategies described in this book, after the age of 75.

INDIVIDUAL SAVINGS ACCOUNTS (ISAS)

You can invest up to £10,680 each year in an investment ISA. From April 2011 this limit will increase annually in line with inflation. Equities and exchange-traded funds (ETF) can be held in an ISA but options and covered warrants cannot. A husband and wife could, between them, invest up to £21,360 p.a. in ISAs. The long-term savings potential could therefore be quite significant.

The main tax benefits of ISAs are that there is no Capital Gains Tax or higher-rate/super-rate tax payable on ISA investments. As with SIPPs, the deemed 10% basic-rate tax charge on dividends cannot be reclaimed. Unlike SIPPS, cash interest in a Stocks and Shares ISA suffers a 20% tax charge, as it is deemed to be cash awaiting investment.

From a long-term investment perspective, ISAs differ from SIPPs in the following ways:

- You can withdraw funds, in part or in full, at any time. ISAs are therefore more flexible than SIPPs.

- There are no tax incentives (e.g. tax-relief) on the amounts invested in ISAs.

- All withdrawals from ISAs are tax free.

ADDITIONAL VOLUNTARY CONTRIBUTIONS (AVCS)

These are designed to allow employees to make additional pension contributions to a company pension scheme, normally into a selection of funds offered by the employer. Tax relief is normally granted at source via the PAYE system. As this book is about managing your own funds rather than selecting managed funds, I will not dwell on the complexities of AVCs here.

The key point which I would like to stress is that, by arrangement with the pension scheme, there are times when you can realise the value of your AVC investments and transfer this value into a self-managed SIPP over which you have much more control.

FINANCIAL SPREAD BETTING

The major tax break with spread betting is that profits do not suffer Capital Gains Tax or any other taxes; profits on spread betting are tax-free.

Correspondingly, you cannot claim tax relief for losses incurred on spread bets.

It is possible for the adventurous to make significant profits through spread betting. But it is very high-risk. I provide more information on spread betting, including a potential spread-bet strategy, in chapter 17.

OTHER ALLOWANCES AND PLANNING DEVICES

CAPITAL GAINS TAX ALLOWANCES

The tax-free allowance on capital gains is £10,100 per year per individual. You can offset losses of the same year against any gains in the calculation of chargeable gains. Any losses which have not been fully absorbed by gains of the same tax year can be carried forward indefinitely to be set against future gains, providing that the loss has been registered with HMRC within four years from the tax year in which they occurred.

Capital gains tax rates are 18% for any gains (less the tax-free allowance) that are absorbed by the headroom available within the basic-rate tax band and 28% for the rest.

INCOME TAX ALLOWANCES

Each individual has a tax-free Income Tax allowance of £7475. The basic-rate tax band (20% on most income) covers the first £35,000 of income over this tax-free allowance. In other words, higher-rate tax does not start until total individual income exceeds £42,475.

FAMILY TAX PLANNING

Family tax planning comes in two stages:

1. PLANNING BETWEEN PARTNERS OR SPOUSES

This requires stable relationships because it involves transferring ownership of assets from one partner/spouse to the other. We have seen above that there are various tax allowances and benefits available to individuals:

- tax-free Income Tax allowance

- basic-rate tax band on income

- capital gains tax allowance

- annual ISA investment allowance

The purpose of family tax planning is to ensure that ownership of assets is distributed between family members to make the most use of tax allowances and benefits. For example, if a husband owns shares on which the dividend income of £42,475 all falls within his higher-rate tax band and his partner has no income at all, he could increase the family income by £10,618 per year, net of tax, by transferring the shares to his wife/civil partner (there is no CGT payable on the transfer of assets to a spouse/civil partner).

The reason for the increased income is that the husband will pay an extra 25% higher-rate tax on the dividend income, whereas the spouse/partner will pay no additional income tax because it all falls within the basic-rate tax band. Similar savings/tax benefits through effective asset distribution can be achieved with respect to CGT and ISAs.

2. TAX-PLANNING FOR CHILDREN

For practical purposes this applies to adult children, since, although minors can hold shares, it is very difficult for them to sell them. Minors can hold ISAs from the age of 15. This type of tax-planning requires a high degree of trust between parent and child, as it involves the parent giving cash to the child on the understanding that it will be held as an investment for the future rather than squandered immediately.

There may be a further understanding (not legally binding) that, should the parents fall on hard times, the child/children will look after them. Cash needs to be given instead of the transference of other assets because the latter may trigger a CGT bill, as also may the sale of assets to realise cash.

There are two potential benefits of this early transfer of cash from parents to child (assuming of course that the parents can live comfortably on their remaining income):

1. The maximised use of tax-free allowances.

2. The early start of the seven-year clock, after which the gift becomes free of inheritance tax.

20

THE BEST SERVICE PROVIDERS

Having established your investment aims you should assemble the platforms and tools required to reach these objectives.

To minimise the effort and cost of managing your own funds, you need to pick good, reliable, inexpensive service providers. All should have online access.

To avoid having large sums of money on current account, earning no interest, you should be able to make financial transfers online on a same-day basis. Many financial institutions make it difficult for you to do this; they make a lot of profit from money lying unrewarded on current accounts. You must make all your assets sweat, by which I mean your investments should be working for you at all times.

You will need all or most of these:

1. a current account

2. an instant-access interest-bearing account

3. an ISA provider, with online dealing

4. a SIPP provider, with online dealing

5. an online broker

6. information on covered warrants

And, to optimise managing a fund of individual shares:

7. ShareMaestro

8. and, ideally, ShareScope

The service providers I mention in this section are those which I have found to offer a good, inexpensive service in their particular field. They all have very good online facilities. However, I have not conducted an exhaustive survey of each market nor have I been paid to recommend any of these service providers.

The costs quoted are those at the time of writing. You need to check the current tariffs before committing to any service. Caveat emptor, as always.

1. CURRENT ACCOUNT

NatWest have an excellent online system. You can view all the balances on your accounts with NatWest in real-time. Any funds received by CHAPS (the high-value same-day payment system) are credited during the day and are shown as soon as they have been credited. NatWest was one of the first banks to introduce Faster Payments, which allows you to make same-day value payments (on business days) for no charge to other financial institutions up to the value of £10,000.

You can also make instant transfers online for any amount between your NatWest accounts (the limit per transfer is £99,999.99, but you can make as many transfers as you like within the balance of the account from which you are making the transfer).

NatWest also offer instant-access interest-bearing accounts and their interest-rates can be competitive. There is no charge for the basic current account service but there is the usual array of charges for specific services used (e.g. a CHAPS payment costs £23).

A current weakness in the service is same-day CHAPS instructions. Very few banks are strong in this area. You can instruct CHAPS payments over the phone, with appropriate security checks, up to £100,000. Over that limit the only same-day instruction option is to instruct by fax (dinosaur technology!), with a fax indemnity in place, or to visit your local NatWest branch.

Another important consideration with banks is financial security, as the FSA compensation limit is only £85,000 per account-holder per eligible institution.

2. INSTANT-ACCESS INTEREST-BEARING ACCOUNT

You can find most of the best current available interest rates at: **www.moneyfacts.co.uk**. I would always prefer some element of interest guarantee, as financial institutions have a nasty habit of sucking you in and then quietly dropping interest rates. You should periodically check the Moneyfacts website to ensure that the rate on your account remains competitive.

3. ISA PROVIDER

Barclays Stockbrokers (**www.stockbrokers.barclays.co.uk**) have a very slick online system, with very easy online dealing facilities, the ability to place stop-loss orders and a full range of instruments tradable within the ISA parameters.

The online transaction history is also very good and the charges are competitive. The basic administration charge, on anything other than cash and funds which pay a renewal commission, is £36 p.a. up to a £7500 portfolio and £60 p.a. for any amount above this, with no limit.

Online dealing charges are £12.95 per online deal, reducing if you are a very frequent trader. There is also a UK-based customer service telephone service, with automated ringback option if the wait period is too long. The Barclays service also integrates the Digital Look research data.

4. SIPP PROVIDER

Hargreaves Lansdown (**www.h-l.co.uk**) provide a good SIPP service with easy online dealing and a recently introduced stop-loss facility. They have a full range of SIPP-tradable instruments, including covered warrants and ETFs.

They tend to offer cash interest rates higher than most SIPP providers and often offer fixed-rate deals. Unusually, they charge no set-up fee for a SIPP. The basic annual administration charge on anything other than cash and funds which pay a renewal commission is 0.5% p.a. of the portfolio, up to a maximum of £200. Online dealing charges are £11.95 per deal or less for frequent trading activity. Additional charges apply for income drawdown and flexible drawdown. I have found the UK-based customer service desk to be very helpful.

5. ONLINE BROKER

For investment outside a tax-free wrapper, Barclays Stockbrokers offer a MarketMaster account, which has the same excellent online facilities as their ISA account. There is a wide range of tradable securities, including equities, ETFs and covered warrants. The online dealing commission structure is the same as for the ISA account but there is a charge of £14.40 for every quarter in which a deal does not occur.

6. COVERED WARRANTS

The main issuers of FTSE100 covered warrants are Société Générale and the Royal Bank of Scotland. Digital Look has a search facility to find the appropriate strike price and expiry date for the covered warrant which you require (at: **www.digitallook.com/dlmedia/investing/covered_warrants**).

To trade a particular covered warrant online with your broker, SIPP or ISA provider, you will need the warrant identifier. You can obtain these identifiers and the current prices from these sources:

• Royal Bank of Scotland (**ukmarkets.rbs.com**)

and

• Société Générale (**www.sglistedproducts.co.uk**).

Both websites also have educational literature about covered warrants.

7. FINANCIAL SPREAD BETTING

I suggest that you test the trading platform of a potential spread betting firm on a fantasy trading basis before committing money to actual trading. You should also check, as far as you can, that the firm is not in danger of imminent collapse. This is a risk, albeit a small one.

There is a large choice of firms. I am not recommending a specific firm but here are a few for you to consider:

• IG Index (**www.igindex.co.uk**). This is the biggest spread betting firm in the UK.

• City Index (**www.cityindex.co.uk**). Another large firm, with a range of trading platforms for mobile phones.

• Tradefair (**www.tradefair.com**).

8. SHAREMAESTRO

ShareMaestro uses a similar share valuation methodology to that detailed in this book. ShareMaestro provides the following advantages to those who wish to manage their own share portfolios:

- Clients can download a weekly data file for processing in ShareMaestro to provide automated valuations of the FTSE100 and of all shares in the FTSE All-Share index (subject to all required data on a share being available). The data file is pre-populated with the necessary data. This saves the effort of keying in data manually for a large number of shares to identify the best and worst value.

- The data file can be customised to provide valuations according to the client's own parameters.

- Bulk share valuation results can be exported to Microsoft Excel to take advantage of Excel's facilities; e.g. shares can be sorted from highest valuation to lowest, or vice-versa.

- Each share valuation is given its own ID and is stored in the ShareMaestro database. It is easy to perform scenario-testing on a specific share valuation by changing the value of input data fields in the share valuation screen, either individually or in combination.

A subscription to ShareMaestro costs £200 p.a. or £18 per month.

9. SHARESCOPE

ShareScope is, by far, the leading subscription-provider of share data to private clients. It regularly wins awards from investment magazines such as the *Investors Chronicle* and *Shares Magazine*. ShareScope provides the following advantages for users of the System:

- You can see the detail of each individual broker forecast which makes up the consensus broker forecast. This enables you to see how many individual forecasts there are and the spread of these forecasts.

- Historic data is available going back to 1994.

- You can screen for shares which meet particular criteria which you can set from a large list of options, e.g. dividend yield, PE ratio and gearing ratio.

- You can set alerts to inform you when particular events are occuring for a share in which you are interested, e.g. price change, directors' dealings, news events.

- You can set up and manage share portfolios, including the calculation of Capital Gains Tax, if applicable.

- ShareScope users can select their own choice of shares (e.g. all shares in a sector) for bulk valuation runs in ShareMaestro.

- A full range of technical analysis charts is available, including moving averages, which are used for risk control in the high-risk strategy described in chapter 17.

ShareScope also has a host of other features.

There are three levels of ShareScope subscription. The basic Gold level includes all the features listed above and costs £195 per year or £18 per month.

21 KEY RISK CONTROLS

Your overall aim should be to maximise the long-term real market value of your savings. Excluding inflation, which you cannot control, there are four key threats to your ability to achieve this aim:

1. third-party fees and management costs

2. poor investment returns

3. tax

4. credit risk.

You can mitigate or eliminate these threats by implementing the key risk controls set out in this chapter.

MANAGE YOUR OWN FUNDS

Apart from poor investment performance, commercial fund management fees are the biggest threat to the real value of your equity savings. Over a 40-year period, your self-managed fund will be worth 93% more than a typical commercially managed fund – purely because you will be avoiding high commercial fund management charges. I hope that this book has shown you how simple and rewarding it can be to manage your own funds.

DO NOT BE A PASSIVE INVESTOR

The long-term track record of the System shows that you should achieve greater returns by investing in the market (or an individual share) when it is good value and disinvesting when it is bad value. The percentage valuations to market are indicators of good or bad value, according to the assumptions which you have made. This policy of being active rather than passive reduces your risk, as you should miss the worst impact of market crashes by being invested in cash.

USE YOUR PARACHUTE

On the very rare occasions when the FTSE100 goes into deep freefall, get out of the market (including selling any shares which you may hold) if you are not already out of it. Within chapter 17 (see pages 193 to 195) I explain a simple way in which you can determine the exit point and also how you can spot when it is safe to get back in the market.

USE STOP-LOSSES

One of the ways in which private investors lose money is by failing to exit in time from a deteriorating situation. It is psychologically very difficult to recognise a loss. When you are sitting on a big loss, there is always the temptation to think that the share will revert at some stage to the price at which you bought it. A disciplined stop-loss strategy can combat this psychological weakness.

I have suggested several ways to use stop-losses, including putting a trailing stop-loss of, say, 12%, on the purchase price of shares you have bought. That way you should avoid massive losses but should also lock-in profits. These stop-losses should be used in conjunction with the valuation signals: i.e. consider selling a share if the valuation percentage to the market price has fallen to a level which shows the current price to be too dear.

It is essential to use stop-losses with the high-risk strategies covered in chapter 17. Otherwise you could rapidly lose all of your investment funds.

INVESTING IN INDIVIDUAL SHARES

Mitigate the risk of investing in individual shares by employing the techniques which I covered in chapter 13, including:

- Spread your risk over at least ten shares covering at least five sectors.
- Never take the default valuations of shares at face value. Undertake due diligence steps before making a decision on whether to invest in the share.

- Keep up with news affecting your shares. Investigate bad news and act if necessary.

- Review the progress of your portfolio at least weekly and follow the financial news daily in case anything occurs which may affect the value of your shares. You can get news alerts specific to your company from Digital Look and ShareScope.

MAKE USE OF TAX BREAKS

Take advantage of the tax breaks covered in chapter 19 to minimise or eliminate the impact of tax on your savings.

MONITOR CREDIT RISK

Investment in, for example, covered warrants, spread bets and structured products, is subject to the risk of default by the institution which is providing or underwriting the investment. You should find out the name of the institution to which you are at risk and avoid/exit the investment if you believe that the institution is at risk of failure.

If you are investing in an ETF, you should first check that 100% of the investment, apart from cash awaiting investment, is in physical securities rather than in derivatives.

Minimise/eliminate credit risk on cash deposits by spreading your investments amongst institutions which are covered by the FSA deposit compensation scheme (maximum £85,000 per institution).

NEVER PUT ALL YOUR EGGS IN A HIGH-RISK BASKET

The high-risk strategies which I have described can, potentially, deliver sparkling rewards but they are called high risk for a reason. You should never bet all your investment savings on a high-risk strategy. Not only do you suffer market risk (albeit mitigated by the risk controls incorporated into the strategy) but you suffer the credit risk described above.

MONITOR THE FTSE 100 DIVIDEND GROWTH TREND

The long-term real growth rate of the FTSE100 dividend has been historically around 2% p.a. Whilst company management and staff are incentivised to ensure that their companies prosper, there is no divine law which states that 2% will continue to be an appropriate long-term yardstick for the FTSE100. There will be occasions, as in 2011, when the five-year economic outlook merits a lower dividend growth figure. If systemic long-term change, supported by a change in the long-term dividend trend, justifies a different default real growth rate, then the System is designed to accommodate this change.

At the time of writing, after declining for three years, the FTSE100 dividend is starting to increase again. It is too early to consign 2% to history as a long-term yardstick. Nevertheless, it may be prudent to use 0% or less as the FTSE100 real dividend growth rate assumption until the FTSE100 has demonstrated 2% real growth over the previous year (on a rolling basis rather than by calendar year).

EPILOGUE

The purpose of this book has been to equip you with the tools, knowledge and enthusiasm to manage successfully your own equity funds. Equities are the only asset class whose price is driven by the results of human enterprise rather than just by supply and demand. I therefore believe that equities will continue to deliver much better real long-term returns than cash and bonds.

Managing your own equity funds can be enjoyable as well as profitable. By now you should understand, both in theory and from its track record, why the System will give you an edge in the market. The threats to your prosperity from reducing pensions and ever-increasing taxes are clear. As a result, for most of us, successful personal fund management will increasingly become an essential skill if we want to secure our financial future.

I wish you every success in your own journey to financial security.

APPENDICES

APPENDIX 1 – FREE WEB INFORMATION SOURCES

FTSE100 AND SHARE VALUATION

All the information which you need to produce default valuations for the FTSE100 and for individual shares, as detailed in chapters 7 and 9, is available free on the internet.

FINANCIAL TIMES

markets.ft.com/research/Markets/Data-Archive

for:

- FTSE100 price
- FTSE100 dividend yield
- redemption yield % p.a. five-year gilts.

BANK OF ENGLAND

www.bankofengland.co.uk/statistics

for:

- average inflation rate

- end-period inflation rate.

DIGITAL LOOK

companyresearch.digitallook.com/cgi-bin/dlmedia/investing/screening_tools/performance_tables

for:

- share price
- share net dividend yield percentage
- actual end-period dividend cover
- real dividend growth rate
- share risk premium.

This service is free but you will have to register.

The Digital Look and *FT* websites also have the information to undertake due diligence checks on companies before making investment decisions, including:

- news flow
- price-to-earnings ratio (PE ratio)
- past and prospective record of earnings and dividends per share
- cash flow per share and cash flow trends
- sales per share and sales trends
- gearing ratio
- interest cover
- current ratio
- directors dealing
- share price momentum
- moving averages.

LIVE SHARE PRICES

Most free sites provide prices which are at least 20 minutes stale. You can get live share prices by using one of the online dealing services but not executing the deal. Alternatively you can get live prices by registering free with ADVFN (at: **www.advfn.com**).

STOCK SCREENER

You can find a great stock screener from the *FT* at: **markets.ft.com/screener/customScreen.asp**

COMPANY REPORT AND ACCOUNTS

You can get copies of reports and accounts on all public companies from the company websites.

FTSE 100 COVERED WARRANT PRICES AND INFORMATION

ROYAL BANK OF SCOTLAND

ukmarkets.rbs.com

SOCIÉTÉ GÉNÉRALE

www.sglistedproducts.co.uk

FINANCIAL SPREAD BET INFORMATION

Information on spread betting can be found at many sites, including Barclays' website: **www.stockbrokers.barclays.co.uk**

ISA INFORMATION

ISA information can also be obtained from Barclays Stockbrokers.

SIPP INFORMATION

SIPP information be found on many sites including Hargreaves Lansdown's website (at: **www.h-l.co.uk**).

BEST CASH DEPOSIT INTEREST RATES

From moneyfacts: **www.moneyfacts.co.uk**

TAX INFORMATION

From HMRC: **www.hmrc.gov.uk**

APPENDIX 2 – GLOSSARY OF TERMS

Further information about these terms can be found by referring to the index and consulting the relevant pages in the book.

ALTERNATIVE INVESTMENT

This term covers a wide range of alternative investments including works of art, antiques, stamps and fine wines. You need specialist knowledge for alternative investments to avoid losing a lot of money.

ANNUITY

Annuities are offered by insurance companies to provide annual income in return for a lump sum investment. The annual income can be fixed or inflation-protected, either up to a set percentage inflation increase each year or to an unlimited percentage. The stronger the inflation protection, the lower the initial annuity amount which you will be offered.

Annuities are commonly used to provide pensions from lump sum pension savings. You are exposed to the risk of the insurance company which provides the annuity defaulting or going bust.

BOND

Companies and governments issue bonds when they wish to raise money. The bonds may have fixed or variable interest rates and some bonds are convertible, converting into shares upon conditions set when the bond is issued.

After the primary sale of the bonds to raise money for the issuing institution, bonds, being securities, are tradable on the secondary market. UK government bonds are called gilts.

CAPITAL GAINS TAX

Under the UK tax regime, Capital Gains Tax is payable on the profit made, less certain sales costs, from the sales of assets. There is an annual allowance of tax-free chargeable gains. Losses can be set off against gains, and losses unused in one year can be set off against gains in future years, providing the loss is notified to HMRC within four years of the loss being made. Further information is available (at: **www.hmrc.gov.uk**).

No Capital Gains Tax is payable on profits made within an ISA or a SIPP.

CASH

Cash is money held on deposit with banks, building societies and other licensed deposit-takers. Interest rates (if any) can be either fixed or variable. Cash is the only asset whose actual value should not fall (except in the very rare instance of negative interest rates). However, the real value can fall and frequently does fall, especially if inflation is high.

CASH FLOW (SEE ALSO FREE CASH FLOW)

Cash flow is the cash generated by a company. Cash flow is earnings adjusted for non-cash items such as depreciation and amortisation.

COMMODITIES

Commodities are generally physical assets such as minerals, metals, vegetables, meat and oil. Commodities are traded in specialist markets and can be traded on a future basis where physical delivery rarely occurs. Commodities investment is high-risk because the supply of many commodities is variable. Gold is particularly speculative because it is regarded as the ultimate long-term safe haven. Its price often rises in response to severe uncertainty caused by major political or other events.

COVERED WARRANT

A covered warrant is issued by a financial institution and entitles the holder to buy or sell specified financial instruments at a specified price by a specified date. The warrants are tradable securities and the market-making firms are often the issuers of the warrants. A covered warrant in equities operates in a very similar way to an equity option. Covered warrants are high-risk investments because, without appropriate risk control, you could lose all of your investment very quickly.

DERIVATIVE

A derivative is a tradable security whose value is dependent, directly or indirectly, on the price of an underlying cash instrument (such as a share or a bond). Options, futures and covered warrants are examples of derivatives.

DISCOUNTED CASH FLOW (DCF)

DCF is used to translate future values into today's values by using, as a discount rate, your required rate of return. It is the reverse procedure from using a compound growth rate to project a future value from today's value. For example, if you wanted to project the future value of £100 in two years' time at a compound growth rate of 20% p.a. you would use the following formula: £100 x 1.2 x 1.2 = £144. If you wanted to calculate the net present value of £144 received in two years' time you would reverse the process. If you used the same 20% as a discount rate, the formula would be £144 x (100 ÷ 120) x (100 ÷ 120) = 100. However, if you applied a lower discount rate, say 10% p.a., the net present value of £144 would be higher: £144 x (100 ÷ 110) x (100 ÷ 110) = £119.

DCF is widely used in investment appraisals, where is it necessary to calculate the present value of an investment which has costs and revenues projected over several years.

DIVIDEND

A dividend is a payment made by a company as a return to its shareholders on their investment in the company. Dividends are normally paid in cash but they can sometimes be paid in the form of additional shares (scrip dividends). Most companies pay an interim dividend and a final dividend, which is announced at the time of the announcement of the full year results. Some large companies pay a quarterly dividend.

DIVIDEND COVER

Dividend cover is the ratio of the company's earnings to its dividend. This cover is commonly used to assess the ability of a company to maintain or increase its dividend in the future. Low dividend covers are therefore normally associated with high dividend yields and vice-versa.

DIVIDEND YIELD

The dividend yield quoted in most share data services is the dividend paid for the latest financial year expressed as a percentage of the current share price. The dividend used for the calculation is the dividend actually paid by the company, which is currently deemed to be net of basic rate tax (10% for dividends). Normally the dividend used to calculate the dividend yield is the total of dividends for the last financial year, including final dividends which have been declared but not yet paid. However, some yield calculations make adjustments for any changes in interim dividends which have been declared for the current financial year.

When a share price goes *ex-dividend* it means that the buyer of the share is not entitled to receive a dividend which has been declared but not yet paid. The dividend is retained by the seller. The ex-dividend date is important for trading in equity derivatives and spread bets. A *prospective* dividend yield normally refers to the total dividend expected to be paid for the current financial year, expressed as a percentage of the current share price.

EARNINGS

A company's earnings are broadly its net profits after tax. Another measure of earnings is EBIT – earnings before interest and tax. Earnings include both cash and non-cash items (e.g. depreciation) and can be massaged to present the company in a favourable light. A study of the company's report and accounts should reveal the extent of the massaging, except when the company directors have been dishonest, fraudulent and/or negligent.

EARNINGS YIELD

The earnings yield is the inverse of the price-to-earnings ratio. It is the earnings per share (normally for the last financial year) expressed as a percentage of the share price.

EQUITIES

Another name for shares.

EXCHANGE-TRADED FUND (ETF)

ETFs are investment funds which trade on stock exchanges. The funds can hold various assets. The ones relevant to this book are those which hold UK equities. ETFs in the FTSE100 and FTSE250 aim to replicate the performance of these indices before charges. They are growing in popularity because:

- They generally have a low cost structure.

- They pay regular dividends.

- Unlike unit trusts and OEICs, you know the price at which you are trading. The spread between the buy and sell price is normally very narrow.

- There is no stamp duty payable on ETF investments.

FREE CASH FLOW

Free cash flow is cash flow with actual capital expenditure deducted. This measure seeks to show the true impact of capital expenditure on current cash flow. It can be misleading in years of exceptionally high or low capital expenditure.

FTSE100 INDEX

The FTSE100 index is the most widely used barometer of the UK stock market. The index includes the top 100 UK shares by market value and accounts for around 81% of the value of the UK stock market. The index is calculated from the share prices of the top 100 companies, weighted by the total market value (share price x total number of shares) of each company.

FTSE250 INDEX

This is the index of the next top 250 shares, weighted by market value, after the FTSE100. The index is calculated in a similar way to the FTSE100 and accounts for about 15% of the value of the stock market.

FTSE ALL-SHARE INDEX

This index comprises companies in the FTSE100 index, the FTSE250 index and the FTSE Small Cap index.

GEARING RATIO

This is a measure of how indebted a company is. The gearing ratio is calculated from total borrowings less cash divided by total equity (capital and reserves).

GILT

A gilt is a bond issued by the UK government to raise funds. Most have fixed redemption dates. There are two types of gilt:

- *Index-linked gilts* where both the interest and the price at which the capital will be redeemed are adjusted to take account of movement in the Retail Price Index (RPI).

- *Ordinary gilts* where the interest rate is fixed in relation to the original par value of the gilt.

After their primary issuance, both types of gilts trade on the secondary market. If interest rates have risen above the level pertaining when the gilt was issued (and on which the interest rate is set), the gilt will normally trade below its issue value. There are two types of yield calculation for ordinary gilts:

- *Current yield* – annual interest payment expressed as a percentage of the current market price.

- *Gross redemption yield* – includes the annual interest payment but also takes into account the gain or loss to be made on redemption date by comparing the current market price with the redemption value and also taking into account the time to redemption. Adjustments are made to market prices to take into account pending interest payments.

INFLATION

Inflation is the annual rate at which prices are increasing. Positive inflation is a measure of the declining purchasing power of money. Very occasionally there is negative inflation, which measures the increasing purchasing power of money when prices are falling.

In the UK, there are various measures of inflation, depending on the selection of goods and services for which the prices are measured. The standard measure of inflation used to be the Retail Price Index (RPI) but governments have increasingly used the Consumer Price Index (CPI) as their preferred measure.

It is no coincidence that the CPI is normally lower than the RPI – as a result, the use of this measure maximises tax revenues and minimises what the government has to pay out in inflation-linked benefits. The CPI excludes major items of expenditure incurred by most households – e.g. mortgage interest.

As I am more concerned with maximising the real value of your savings in actual rather than presentational terms, I have used the RPI (all items) to calculate the real returns of the FTSE100 strategies covered in this book.

INTEREST COVER

Interest cover is earnings before interest and tax divided by the interest charge for a company. It is a measure of how well positioned a company is to service its debt.

INTRINSIC VALUE

In the context of this book, intrinsic value is a calculation of the real current investment value of a share. Intrinsic value contrasts with the current market price, which is the price at which the share is trading at a particular moment in time.

INDIVIDUAL SAVINGS ACCOUNT (ISA)

ISAs are savings accounts that are free from Income Tax and Capital Gains Tax. There are two types of ISAs – Cash ISAs and Stocks and Shares ISAs.

Within a Stocks and Shares ISA, dividend income is free from higher-rate tax but you cannot reclaim the basic rate tax deducted at source on dividends. Cash interest in a Stocks and Shares ISA is also subject to basic-rate tax (but not higher-rate tax). Unlike SIPPs, there is no tax relief granted on funds invested in an ISA. However, there is no tax deducted on any cash withdrawn from an ISA.

LIQUIDITY

Liquidity is a measure of a company's ability to meet its short-term obligations. However profitable a company may be, it could go to the wall if it cannot meet its short-term obligations. The current ratio is aimed at assessing the liquidity health of a company. It measures the relationship of current assets to current liabilities.

MOMENTUM/RELATIVE MOMENTUM

In share investing, momentum is the pace at which a share or index price is rising or falling. There are various ways of measuring this momentum, including moving averages (see below). Relative momentum is the pace of movement in a share price compared with, for example, its industry sector or the market as a whole.

Various short-term trading strategies incorporate momentum, as momentum can be a good indicator of future short-term price movement. However momentum is not normally a good indicator of future long-term price movement.

MOVING AVERAGE

A moving average smooths out day-to-day price fluctuations with the aim of showing the price trend of a share. There are different ways to calculate moving averages. We need only concern ourselves here with the *simple moving average*. This is the sum of prices over a specific number of days, divided by that number of days. Moving averages are normally plotted as lines on a graph. Several of the internet sources mentioned in this book will create moving average graphs online from parameters which you set.

Some trading systems use two different moving averages (e.g. 50-day and 90-day) to detect turning points in the market, where the two lines cross.

NET ASSET VALUE (NAV)

The net assets of a company are total assets less total liabilities. Net assets are the accounting value of the stake in the company owned by shareholders. Net assets are hence often expressed in terms of net assets per share. In the early days of value investing, Benjamin Graham would look for companies whose share prices were considerably below the Net Asset Value (or book value) per share. Now hardly any companies meet this criterion. The share price focus is much more on the potential for future earnings and dividend streams.

NET PRESENT VALUE

See *discounted cash flow*.

OEICS (OPEN-ENDED INVESTMENT COMPANIES)

To an investor, OEICS are very similar to unit trusts. They are collective investments in which you purchase shares rather than units, and the share prices are determined by the net asset values of the OEICs. The initial charges, management fees and range of funds are very similar to those of unit trusts and you can also only deal on a forward pricing basis. The main difference is that there is only one dealing price for an OEIC and therefore no bid/offer spread. However, there are sometimes penalties for early redemption of the shares once purchased.

PRICE/EARNINGS TO GROWTH (PEG) RATIO

The PEG ratio for a company is the ratio of the prospective price-to-earnings ratio (price per share divided by earnings per share) to the prospective earnings growth rate (normally over the next 12 months).

The PEG ratio is designed to be a measure of the value of the share price. The lower the ratio the better. I discuss my reservations about this measure in chapter 3.

PRICE-TO-EARNINGS (PE) RATIO

The PE ratio is the current price per share, divided by the earnings per share (normally the earnings per share for the last financial year).

PRICE-TO-SALES RATIO

This is the current share price divided by the sales per share (normally for the last financial year).

RETAIL PRICE INDEX

See *inflation*.

RISK PREMIUM

In the context of this book, the risk premium is the extra return demanded by investors for accepting the greater risk of investing in a share as opposed to investing in a gilt, which is virtually risk-free, if you ignore inflation and hold the gilt to redemption. Normally the risk premium is expressed as an additional percentage return required for each year of investment. My valuation system accounts for the risk premium by discounting the total future projected investment value in five years' time. On this basis, 10% has been tested to be appropriate for a five-year investment in the FTSE100.

The risk premium required for an individual company investment is much harder to assess. Whilst, barring Armageddon, you will not lose all your investment in a FTSE100 ETF, your investment in an individual company, even a FTSE100 company, could become worthless. Different approaches to calculating company risk premiums were discussed in chapter 9.

SELF-INVESTED PERSONAL PENSION (SIPP)

SIPPs enable individuals to build up personal pension funds with tax-free growth. There are also tax incentives for SIPP investments. Withdrawals from SIPPs cannot be made until a pension is drawn from the SIPP. SIPPs were covered in detail in chapter 19. The rules are complicated and so you should consult a professional pensions adviser before investing in a SIPP.

SIPPs could be a very useful vehicle for some of your investments. You can hold a wide range of investments in a SIPP.

SHARES

Shares are issued by companies to raise funds as an alternative to borrowing money. A company can issue various types of shares, with different rights and obligations, but the most commonly traded share is the *ordinary share.*

A company may, but is not obliged to, pay regular dividends to ordinary shareholders as a return on their investment. The company's ability to pay dividends is heavily influenced by the earnings which it makes.

If a company is wound up, the shareholders will share the residual value of the company (if any) after all its debts and obligations have been met in proportion to the number of shares which they hold.

SPREAD BETS

Financial spread bets are high-risk investments. As far as equities are concerned, you can bet on the future price movement of a share or of the FTSE100. At any one time there is a buy price and a sell price, with a spread in between. The spread is the profit of the spread bet provider. This spread is similar to the spread between the buy and sell price provided by a market-maker of a share, but it also covers the commission of the spread-bet firm. If you buy at the prevailing buy price and subsequently sell at the prevailing sell price, your profit (or loss) is the difference between the two prices multiplied by the amount of stake which you have bet for each point of price movement.

One of the reasons why spread bets are high-risk is that you can use heavy leverage – i.e. get an exposure to the market which is many times greater than the amount of cash which you have to deposit initially. This leverage magnifies profits and losses greatly.

Spread bet profits are not subject to Capital Gains Tax.

STRUCTURED PRODUCTS

There are various types of structured products, which are issued by financial institutions. The ones relevant to this book are those which provide a variable cash return dependent on the performance of the FTSE100. Chapter 16 looked at how the System can be used to assess the merits of investing in a FTSE100-linked structured product.

TECHNICAL ANALYSIS

Technical analysis seeks to predict future price movements from past price movements and, in some cases, from trading volumes. I discuss how technical analysis differs from value investing in chapter 4.

TRACKER FUND

An equity tracker fund aims to reproduce the performance of an index, such as the FTSE100, as closely as possible. The fund achieves this tracking by buying the constituent shares of the index in proportion to their weighting within the index. Tracker funds generally have lower costs than actively managed funds because there is no research or decision-making required in the selection of companies within the fund.

UNIT TRUSTS

Unit trusts are collective investments in which investors buy units. The price of each unit reflects the number of units in issue and the Net Asset Value of the trust. Unit trusts are established for different markets and products so that investors can gain exposure to the security group of their choice (e.g. UK Smaller Companies).

In addition to buy/sell spreads, unit trusts normally have initial charges of around 5%, although much of this charge can be avoided by buying through a discount broker. The management fees of actively managed funds (as opposed to index-tracking funds) are around 1.5% p.a., with other costs increasing total annual costs to at least 1.8% p.a. In addition to these high charges, what I most dislike about unit trusts is the fact that you can only deal once a day, and then only on a forward basis so that you never know the price at which you are dealing. This is not a recipe for smart investment decisions.

VALUE INVESTING

Value investing is the polar opposite of investing on the basis of technical analysts. Value investors believe that fundamental financial and other factors determine whether the share price of a company offers good value or poor value and, therefore, whether the share price is likely to increase or decrease. Value investors generally have a medium- to long-term investment horizon, since it can sometimes take three or more years for a company's share price to reach fair value.

INDEX